D1538616

HURRICANE ISLAND

THE TOWN THAT DISAPPEARED

HURRICANE ISLAND

THE TOWN THAT DISAPPEARED

Eleanor Motley Richardson

with an Introduction by Philip W. Conkling

ISLAND INSTITUTE

Rockland, Maine

in cooperation with **Hurricane Island Outward Bound School**

Published by the Island Institute
Rockland, Maine

Library of Congress Catalog Card Number 89-84724

ISBN 0-942-719-08-5

Book and cover by AMY FISCHER DESIGN
Cover photo by Eleanor Motley Richardson
Typeset by Typeworks, Belfast, Maine
Edited by Mike Brown

For more copies of this book, call or write:

Eleanor M. Richardson
P.O. Box 1843
Andover, MA 01810
978/470-1006

To my mother
Catharine Little Motley
who dropped everything one October day in 1963
and took me to Hurricane

and her mother
Eleanor Wheeler Little
(1892–1988)
who blessed the project at its beginning
but did not live to see its completion

and her mother
Ellen Hayward Wheeler
(1860–1958)
who brought us all
to the Fox Islands

The St. Louis Post Office and Federal Building, designed by Alfred Bult Mullett and James G. Hill, was built from 1874-1884. It was the first major contract for the Hurricane Granite Company, whose stone comprises the upper stories. Photo by Robert C. Pettus, courtesy Landmarks Association of St. Louis, Inc., which together with the committee S.T.O.P. (Save the Old Post Office) and the American Institute of Architects helped save the Post Office from destruction in the 1960s.

Contents

Rockport

WEST PENOBSCOT BAY

North Haven

Rockland

Owls Head

Vinalhaven

MUSCLE RIDGE CHANNEL

High Island

Spruce Head

Dix Island

Hurricane Island

LOCATOR MAP

Acknowledgments

THE RESEARCHER OF HURRICANE ISLAND'S history will find scant published information. By far, the greatest resource is people. My thanks to the following people who have been especially helpful in this quest:

Peter T. Richardson, for his many photographs and historical photo copying, and for his constant support of this project; Margaret Philbrook Smith, of Eliot, for sharing her life. And Sharon Philbrook, town clerk, Vinalhaven, Maine, for putting me in touch with "Aunt Margaret." Also Buz Tripp, Jamien Morehouse and the Hurricane Island Outward Bound School, for generously sharing their photo collections and knowledge. Mary Olson of Vinalhaven, Min Chilles' daughter, for editing the material on her mother, and Margaret Engelhart, Plattsburgh, N.Y. and Vinalhaven, for talking me into writing this book.

In addition, I would like to thank Kay Davis, Maine State Museum, Augusta; Roy Heisler and Esther Bissell, Vinalhaven Historical Society; Robert N. Davis, Curator, Shore Village Museum, Rockland; Janet Welch, Kennebunk Free Public Library, and the library staffs in Rockland and the Maine State Archives in Augusta; Dick Dooley and Raymond Gross, *Courier Gazette*, Rockland; Elizabeth

Facing page: Spruces in the cellar hole of the Nichols boarding house are no longer young. The building was immense, requiring mid-floor supports such as this. Photo by Eleanor Richardson.

Hurricane's Granite Quarry in 1988. After its abandonment, the quarry filled with fresh water, and it was known to provide excellent fishing. Cruisers and picnickers enjoyed the relatively warm water for swimming. By 1988, a ladder at the base of the rockface testified to the presence of Outward Bound. Photo by Eleanor Motley Richardson

Biddle-Jennings, Marilyn Solvay and Mary Wascott of the Farnsworth Museum, Rockland; Karen Womer, Down East Books, Camden, and Charles McLane.

Other individuals and "family members" who assisted with the book are Beverly Joe Queenin, daughter of John (Giovanni) Ernest Piatti of Hurricane; Walter Hutchinson, Vinalhaven; Marcia Rowling and Ruth Philbrook, Rockland; Judy Larkin, Newton, Mass.; John and Bernadette Luxton, Vinalhaven; Wyman Philbrook, Vinalhaven; Ruth Wade, West Rockport; Leland Overlock, Warren and Susan St. John-Rheault, Owls Head.

And finally, my thanks to the publication team of Philip Conkling, Caitlin Owen Hunter and Julie Canniff of the Island Institute; Mike Brown, editor; Amy Fischer, designer, and Cathy Kasza and Penn Williamson of the Hurricane Island Outward Bound School.

Introduction

by
Philip W. Conkling

ALL AROUND THE GLOBE ARE thousands of small islands where people
arrived to begin new lives sustained by little more than the fragile offerings of
all remote islands. Some colonies have succeeded, but the record, if someone
kept one, would show that a vast number of island communities – often entire
cultures – have simply disappeared.

  One cold, gray morning I came ashore on Hurricane Island, and ultimately
spent the better part of three years cataloging the natural history of this and
surrounding islands. It didn't take long to begin wondering about Hurricane's
past. Large remnants of it, in the form of stone blocks, columns and rusting
machinery, were strewn around the island, only partially hidden by spruce and
alder thickets. Gradually some deeper stories of the place worked their way to
the surface of the imagination. A little lilac grove off the beaten path was
redeemed from the dark forest and bloomed to life; a network of wells and
drainage channels cut in bedrock revealed a complex water works system, as
carefully laid out as those by the Romans; and in the most remote interior loca-
tions, scores of small granite outcrops that had been worked by single individuals

for paving stones lay in quiet contrast to the industrial archaeology of the massive granite works along the southern cliffs.

Who were these people? Where did they come from, and where did they go? It's remarkable, really, how little we know about and appreciate the granite period of Maine coast history. It spanned more than a century, and brought tens of thousands of immigrants to communities on Maine's remote island shores, from Friendship to Jonesport, to carve new lives and dreams from cold stone.

Hurricane's story is perhaps the most poignant of all the granite islands. The quarries of Vinalhaven were bigger and more productive, as were those of Mt. Desert Island. The Dix Island and High Island quarries in the Muscle Ridge left legacies as impressive as those of Hurricane's in the way of effort and output, but nowhere else along the granite coast did so many people of such talent and enterprise disappear literally overnight, leaving behind stone cold records and a few ghosts we are only beginning to recognize.

I caught a whisper of one of the thousands of Hurricane's untold stories one night with just enough moon for walking around – something special in a place with no lights and only owlish night life. I was sitting on one of the moon-bleached bare patches of granite in the village "downtown" running my hand over the rock. I began to feel a straight ridge in the time-smoothed granite surface and with fingers moving faster, I leaned down to adjust my eyes to the moon glow and could just barely make out four letters: 'R' 'P' and 'L', 'M' or 'N'. A tryst discovered a century later. Even more remarkable, the letters had not been chiseled down into the sloping outcrop, rather the granite surrounding the letters had been lovingly worn away – perhaps worried away – leaving these four initials to rise out in quarter inch relief from the hard stone surface. In some ineffable way, finding those unknown initials that night on the small ledge in the middle of what had been the village of Hurricane Island, encapsulated all the poignance of the island town that disappeared.

In this book, Eleanor Richardson has assembled much of what is officially known about Hurricane Island's granite past. Even more important she has recovered a few more of the voices of Hurricane before they, too, are lost in the sounds of the rising rote on these outer shores. I hope this will not be the last word on this impressive place or period of Maine's maritime industrial past.

Author's Preface

MY FATHER ALWAYS TOOK HIS two-week vacation on the island of North Haven, Maine, even though it meant visiting his in-laws. He loved North Haven because he loved sailing almost more than eating. And in North Haven the sole form of transportation getting to and from the island was over the water.

I guess I must have been about five years old the first time they took me to Hurricane Island. It had to be a very fine day for them to choose that island for a picnic because it was a long sail and a cold destination.

They brought the old knockabout in from the mooring and started stowing picnic baskets, warm sweaters and life jackets. I liked the knockabout because it had a tiny cabin where a child could crawl in out of the wind and play house.

My older brother cast off, the sails flapped around for a bit in the doldrums under the spruce-fragrant hill, and then a gentle breeze filled the sails. We beat up the Thoroughfare to the westward, toward the Camden Hills which stood out in vivid blue against the summer sky. At the mouth of the Thoroughfare, we bore off to the southward on a broad reach through Leadbetter's Narrows.

Hurricane Isle, Me.

The town of Hurricane Isle, Maine, from a contemporary postcard. This is the most publicized view of the village. The house at left with a picket fence belonged to superintendent Landers.

As we drifted out of the lee of the smaller islands in the flat morning air, I had my first glimpse of Hurricane. To my surprise, it didn't look like a "cane" at all, but rather like a large green hill covered with pointed green spruces floating in the middle of blue water covered with sunlit sparkles.

A brisk reach across Hurricane Sound brought us to the old wharf where we could tie up the knockabout to the mossy posts without having to drop anchor. The picnic baskets and bathing suits were quickly handed up and I tested out the gripping power of my new red Keds on the slippery ladder while fighting the bulk of my large orange life jacket.

We walked the southern rim of the island to the quarry with its still, green water and its striking, many-faceted cliff of grayish-pink granite rising out of the water on the far side. Here we could swim much more pleasantly than in the ocean as the water was warmer and fresh.

After swimming, we feasted on peanut butter sandwiches, hard-boiled eggs and warm ginger ale. Then, while the older ones climbed to the top of the cliff, my mother took me back around the hill to its grassy eastern slope. The few clusters of little granite blocks were all that was left of the foundations of houses which had once stood there. Four granite fence posts marked off the churchyard. But there was no church. An apple tree arched gracefully over two granite doorsteps – and I climbed the two steps to nowhere. I tried to imagine other children playing on those steps long ago. There were occasional pieces of rusted machinery. The bleached grass was warm and sleepy in the summer sunshine. Members of our party and other picnickers wandered randomly around searching for artifacts from the vanished island community.

After an hour or two on the island, we all rolled back down the hill and boarded the knockabout for the long sail back to North Haven. An afternoon sailing breeze had come up, as it almost always does in the islands, and the slender boat sliced through the waves as we ran home before the wind.

That evening, when we all were bathed and changed for dinner, my grandfather drew me aside and reached for a small picture on the wall. He brought it down close for me to see. "That's Hurricane," he said. It looked very strange. The trees were gone and dozens of straight little white houses covered the hillside. I saw a little city. Back there in the grassy field, I had imagined maybe four or five houses dotting the hill, but this teeming community bore absolutely no resemblance to the sleepy place I had seen that afternoon. It took a long leap of faith, many more picnics, and a good deal of personal research before I grew to understand what it was that had happened on Hurricane Island.

HURRICANE ISLAND

CHAPTER ONE

The Regime of General Davis Tillson

"Lord of the Isles"

1870–1880

TO REACH THE FOX ISLANDS of Penobscot Bay, you board a boat in Rockland, either one of the Maine State Ferry boats, or a private boat. If you choose the ferryboats, the wharves and odors of the mainland fall quickly away behind, and you smell only diesel fumes and saltwater as you pass by the lighthouse on the end of the Rockland Breakwater, head out into the bay and bear off slightly to the south toward the islands. If it's a good day, after about a half hour the land mass ahead of you becomes clearer and you become aware that there is a large island to port and a scattering of smaller islands to starboard. The farthest of these to starboard, and the highest, sitting proudly in the silver path of the morning sun is Hurricane.

Some say it was named Hurricane because the day George Vinal bought the island a hurricane struck. Others think it was named for its exposed position; buffeted by gale winds coming straight across from Spain. No one really knows. Whichever, Hurricane Island stands higher than the others because its core is a great pillar of granite, a mountaintop in the sunken valley of the Penobscot River, depressed below sea level ten thousand years ago by the glaciers.

Facing page: General Davis Tillson in Civil War dress, from an engraving entitled "Brevet Major-General Davis Tillson, formerly Drill Master, Rockland City Guards." Courtesy Shore Village Museum.

"Home built by Tillson on Middle Street (now Talbot) before the Civil War. The Tillsons later moved to an immense Greek Revival house at the corner of Middle and Main streets." From **Shore Village Story, an Informal History of Rockland, Maine,** *published by the Bicentennial Commission, 1976.*

On January 18, 1870, three men purchased Great Hurricane Island from Deborah L. Ginn of Vinalhaven for the sum of $1,000 although it's hard to understand why anyone would want to buy such an exposed rugged island in the coldest month of the year. They didn't buy it for its green carpet of spruces, or the way the morning sun hit the water, or the way the golden grass on the hillside swayed in the sun on a summer afternoon. These men bought the island because they saw an opportunity in Hurricane's big pinkish-grey mountain of stone. The deed conveyed "unto the said [Davis] Tillson one undivided half and to said Patrick McNamara and Garrett Coughlin each one undivided one quarter" of the island.

Although Hurricane was purchased by three men, the driving force behind the deal was General Davis Tillson of Rockland. For the next 19 years, the names of Tillson and Hurricane would be be synonymous. Although Tillson was a man of many ventures and many achievements, Hurricane was at the heart of his endeavors. A portrait of the community that sprouted from that rock is a portrait of a vision inside one man's head. And Tillson was accustomed to making his visions become real. It is therefore necessary to understand the man in order to understand the evolution of the town of granite that grew up to be Hurricane Island.

During his regime, Tillson came to be called "Lord of the Isles" by the Scottish

The Tillson house today. Note the size of the trees. The house of red brick, with fanciful Victorian gingerbread, was built on land that was part of Tillson's father's farm.

granite workers, and "Bombasto Furioso" by the Italian quarrymen who came to Hurricane. And it is rumored that during one election Tillson told his men to vote Republican – or else. When one man cried out, "But it's against the law," Tillson replied, "I own this island and will be master here." During his life the pro-labor *Rockland Opinion* newspaper saw Tillson as an oppressor, imprisoning his workers politically and economically in a company town. Their paychecks went directly into an account at the company store. The fruit of their labors went directly back into company profits. The pro-management *Rockland Gazette* saw Tillson quite differently as the creator of an almost Utopian community where all worked together, labor and mangement alike, for the common good. In fact, Tillson had covered a lot of ground in the forty years before he purchased Hurricane Island in 1870, and his formative years give us some clue as to the two faces of the General and why Hurricane became the town it was.

Davis Tillson was born in Rockland, Maine on April 17, 1830, the son of William F. Tillson of Rockland and Jane (Davis) Tillson of Union, Maine. His mother gave her son the Davis family name, but had little time for him before she died leaving him a half-orphaned only child. His father, a farmer on the western edge of town, remarried when the child was three. Tillson's paternal grandfather, William, was the owner of an inn at Brown's Corner, then part of nearby Thomaston, and a veteran of the Revolutionary War. Davis followed his grandfather's career more closely than his father's. His grandfather lived in the same town with him until the boy was eleven so we may surmise that the older man had considerable influence on his grandson.

Davis Tillson was a hard worker and did well in school. He was accepted by the U.S. Military Academy at West Point, N.Y., entering in 1849. But an unfortunate accident interrupted his military career. During his first semester, a large part of his time at West Point was spent in the hospital due to an problem with his foot. His injury was so severe that ultimately he had to have most of his foot amputated. Amazingly, following a furlough for recovery, he was readmitted to the Academy on the merit of his excellent first semester record. No sooner did he resume his studies, however, than his father died and he had to return home again to settle the estate and "arrange his business affairs." Apparently, either his father or his grandfather had left more than a farm to him in Rockland, Maine.

After returning to Rockland, he resigned himself to leaving the military and turned his energies toward civilian life. He married Margaret E. Achorn, the daughter of Michael Achorn of Rockland, on August 4, 1852, and on October 1, 1856, their first daughter, Jennie, was born. Engineering had always interested him and there was ample opportunity for civil engineering in Midcoast Maine's extensive limestone quarries.

About 1858, he contracted to drain the Ulmer quarries for the White Limerock company in Rockland, a heavy engineering project which required the excavation of large quantities of earth. It took more than a year to complete. It was a highly successful project and he displayed great engineering ability in the work. He received some $20,000 for the project but it was not especially profitable to him. Other enterprises soon brought him in a modicum of wealth, however. In particular he showed excellent judgment in the purchase of mineral lands and in the development of limerock quarries on them from which accumulated a considerable amount of money.

In the course of his dealings, he made enough of a name for himself so that in 1857 his townsmen elected him to the state legislature. He entered politics just as the Republican Party was being formed and his unflagging allegiance with that party lasted for the rest of his life. His climb in politics was swift. He was made Adjutant General of Maine in 1858 and was an ardent supporter of Samuel Fessenden who was elected to Congress in 1860. On the advice of Fessenden, President Lincoln, soon after his inauguration in 1861, appointed Tillson to the lucrative position of the Collector of Customs for the Waldoboro District. But the Civil War broke out within a year of his appointment and Tillson could not resist the call to the military. He organized the Second Maine Battery of Light Artillery and entered the service on November 1, 1861, as its captain. His brother-in-law covered his custom's position for him back home for nearly a year. By then,

Tillson was already a general and had to relinquish the position to devote his full energies to war.

Due to trouble with the English over the "Trent Affair," he and his men were compelled to stay over the first winter at Fort Preble in Portland. Captain Tillson put the time to good use giving his men intensive training which was to stand them in good stead when the battalion joined the Army of the Rappahanock under Major General Irvin McDowell in April of 1862.

The *Cyclopaedia of American Biography* summarizes Tillson's Civil War career as follows:

> On 22 May, he was promoted [to] major and made chief of artillery in Gen. Edward O.C. Ord's division. After the battle of Cedar Mountain, 9 Aug., 1862, he was assigned to Gen. McDowell's staff as chief of artillery, in which capacity he served during the three days' artillery fight at Rappahannock Station, and then at the second battle of Bull Run.
>
> Subsequently, until April, 1863, he was inspector of artillery, and in January was made lieutenant-colonel, and on 29 March was ordered to Cincinnati, having been commissioned brigadier-general to date from 29 Nov., 1862, and made chief of artillery for fortifications in the Department of the Ohio. He had charge of the defences of Cincinnati and the works on the Louisville and Nashville railroad, and raised and organized two regiments of heavy artillery.
>
> In December, 1863, he was ordered to Knoxville, Tenn., where he supervised various works and was given a brigade in the 23rd army corps, which he commanded in several engagements with Confederate cavalry and irregular troops during the winter of 1863–4. He continued in charge of the works in this district, which were officially commended as the best in the military division of the Mississippi, and also organized the first U.S. heavy artillery of colored troops and the 3rd North Carolina mounted infantry.
>
> Subsequently he had command of the District of East Tennessee until early in 1865, when he was transferred to the 4th division of the Department of the Cumberland, and held that command until the close of the war.
>
> He then offered his resignation; but his services were retained [his resignation was not accepted] and he remained on duty until 1 Dec., 1866, in charge of the freedmen's bureau at Memphis, and subsequently in Georgia. For a year he remained in Georgia after his resignation, engaged in cotton-planting, but then disposed of his interests there and returned to Rockland, Me. where he has since been engaged in the granite business.

You will remember that the man with this brilliant military career had only one foot.

Upon his return to Rockland after the war, and before becoming engaged in the granite business, Tillson opened a lime quarry in Rockland with Orris B. Ulmer which was an immediate success. He then sold the property at a good price as he saw opportunities opening in the granite business. At this time, his second

Rockland office of the Hurricane Granite Company. Pictured at left is Mr. Orris Andrews of Rockland, and at right, Mr. William Hyde. Photo courtesy Shore Village Museum.

daughter, Monira D. Tillson, was born in Rockland. She was 14 years younger than Jennie. Not only the Civil War but possibly the General's "workaholic" nature had something to do with the age gap between his children.

The years following the Civil War were years of prosperity in the North and a time of great patriotism which manifested itself, among other things, in the erection of great monuments and public buildings. Federal contracts for these buildings abounded and granite was the construction material of choice. The selection of a quarry site on an uninhabited island 12 miles offshore was not so illogical as it might seem today. Shipping by schooner down the coast of Maine was at that time by far the most efficient means of transportation. Besides, Tillson not only had the government connections, the businessman's vision and the engineering capabilities to carry out his scheme, but he had also learned in the army how to mobilize men in a hurry.

Hurricane Island in 1870 was little more than a spruce-covered desolate island, the highest of a group of islands off the west shore of Vinalhaven. It was about a mile long and three quarters of a mile wide. It had never supported a settlement although at times a few fishermen had lived on the island. A foundation and well pre-dating the granite settlement was at the northern tip of the island with a small graveyard testifying to at least one previous year-round resident whose identity remains a mystery today. A shell heap and arrowheads offer evidence of still earlier occupants.

According to the research of Charles B. McLane in his book, *Islands of the Mid-Maine Coast*, Hurricane Island was first mentioned by name in a 1772 deed when it was sold with eight other neighboring islands from William Heard to James Heard. The island changed hands many times in the intervening years until George Vinal sold the island to Joseph Ginn in 1852. After Deborah Ginn sold it to Davis Tillson and his partners in 1870, the island stayed in the Tillson family for 50 years.

The 1870 purchase was not the end of the real estate wheeling and dealing, however. Between 1870 and 1875, there were no fewer than eight separate trans-actions as Tillson gradually bought out his partners and used his equity in the island to raise capital for his Hurricane Island granite business. A silent partner, W.C. Kingsley of Brooklyn, N.Y., came into the picture as soon as December, 1870, investing funds in exchange for a share in the business.

By March, 1875, Tillson was able to sell one quarter interest in Hurricane to Kingsley for $37,500. The sum was to be paid back in installments on a regular schedule. The terms of the deed state that the transfer of property will be void if the payment schedule is met. Presumably it was and full ownership reverted to Tillson. Although a newspaper article in *The Rockland Opinion* of July 6, 1877, referred to the fact that "Tillson's property was not held in his own name," no one afterward questioned Tillson's sole ownership of the island.

The business did well from the beginning. In 1874, Tillson invited the Repub-lican triumvirate of Secretary Delano, Maine Senator Hannibal Hamlin and Representative Eugene Hale to visit the island. They were reportedly astonished at the transformation in just four years. The business was worth $100,000, the population of the island was 1,100 or 1,200 and there were 50 dwellings. (Although this figure works out to 24 people per dwelling it could be assumed

that many workers were either housed in boarding houses or commuted from other islands.) A large new polishing mill was under construction. A few years later the Maine Register for 1877 reports a population of 600 and an evaluation of $46,941. Whether or not Tillson had exaggerated the numbers for his visitors in 1874, there is no doubt that they found a thriving community. In 1877, some 255 workers were engaged in contracts for the St. Louis Post Office and the Fall River, Mass., Post Office. Others worked in monument carving. The wages varied from $1 to $3.75 per day and depended on the type of work and on whether or not it was a government contract. Those employed in carving were the most skilled workers and were paid the most followed by those who cut the rough granite from the granite cliffs. At the end of the pay scale were largely unskilled quarry workers who did most of the manual work on the cliffs.

Above: Large cranes with multiple guy wires were used to hoist the granite blocks around the quarry site. By the time this picture was taken, horses were being used, rather than oxen, as draft animals. Photo courtesy HIOBS.

Facing page: The quarry worker in the foreground demonstrates a hand drill, pounded with a mallet, turned, and pounded again to drill a hole. This system was later replaced with steam drills. Photo courtesy HIOBS.

During the 1870s, steady work depended on the letting of contracts for new government buildings. Tillson had total control over what he paid his men – and when. But in March, 1877, workers from four quarries – Spruce Head, Clark Island, Vinalhaven and Hurricane – united to form the first Granite Cutters' Union. Complaints were lodged against General Davis Tillson and others that "contractors were holding back pay, and compelling them to spend it all in company stores." At the Bodwell Granite Company (founded in 1871 on Spruce Head) men worked a ten-hour day, Monday-Friday, and nine hours on Saturdays.

A powerful labor movement had begun which by the early 20th Century, was to number three unions: The Granite-Cutters' Union, the Paving Cutters' Union and the Quarry Workers' Union. With the formation of the unions came a voice strong enough to be heard by those in government who let the contracts. Tillson must have sensed that total control of his world on Hurricane was changing. As early as spring, 1879, Congressman T.H. Murch introduced a bill for an 8-hour day, a move far ahead of his time. Another bill condemned the "Fifteen percent contracts" which guaranteed contractors 15% profits on their gross expenditures. In June, 1877, a delegation from the newly-formed union went to Washington, unbeknown to Tillson, and laid a set of grievances before President Hayes himself.

According to Roger Grindle's history of the granite industry (which is now out of print) "the president politely gave them to understand that they had better return home and that everything should be arranged satisfactorily to all. This was not what the delegates had come to Washington for, however. Such palaver answers for the Indians of the West when they come to interview the Great Father, but not for a couple of shrewd Yankees." They then went to see the Secretary of the Treasury at once.

The delegates demanded to see copies of the new contracts and the secretary refused, but said that the union men would have a hearing before the contracts were finalized. An interchange from that hearing, between Oliver P. Clark of Hurricane, and Lieutenant-Colonel Casey of the Engineer Corps was reported in the pro-labor *Rockland Opinion* regarding the allegations that the quarry owners (who came to be known as the Granite Ring) routinely submitted payrolls listing men working on government projects when in fact they were working on private contracts. The *Rockland Opinion* account noted that: "Mr. Clark offered to make oath that he had himself done so. Col. Casey thought he had got a point on him and the following dialogue ensued:

Casey: So, there you knew that the company was perpetrating a fraud on government when you signed?
Clark: Yes.

Casey: Do you understand that you were an accessory to the fraud, by so doing?
Clark: No; I was obliged to do so in order to get my pay.
Casey: Why did you not protest?
Clark: I did protest.
Casey: To whom?
Clark: To the foreman, I called his attention to the matter and told him that it was irregular.
Casey (after a pause): Did you protest to no one else?
Clark: Yes, I did.
Casey: To whom?
Clark: To the *President of the United States*.
Casey: In what manner?
Clark: By letter, giving a full statement of the matter.
Casey: If you wrote such a letter as that, it is probably on file.
Clark: Probably—*unless it has been destroyed*.

The visit of the delegates to Washington and the unexpectedly complete case they presented, has been a bomb-shell in the camp of the contractors, and they are flying around in dismay. If only the men will be true to themselves now, the prospect is excellent that the work will be done by the government, and they will get fair wages and receive their pay every month, and "not be obliged to spend it at the company store."

Tillson was furious that the men should go to the government behind his back. But on June 27, the granite workers sent the following telegram:

To Hon. John Sherman, Secretary of the Treasury: The workmen on Hurricane Island employed in preparing stone for the St. Louis custom-house and post-office have signed the pay-rolls for May; but Gen Davis Tillson, in the most insulting language, has refused to pay them another dollar. Therefore, the workmen have refused to sign the pay-rolls for June until they have some guarantee that they will receive their pay for May, which is justly their due and which they very much need; and we therefore respectfully ask that you direct the same to be paid by Gen. Tillson, as we believe he has received the money from the government to pay the same, and which he is unjustly and illegally withholding from us, to our great loss and inconvenience.

The *Opinion*, publishing during an era when many newspapers made little pretense of objective journalism, reported Tillson's response:

"Garrulous Tillson":

Like a driveling, loquacious old woman, the public functionary who styles himself King of Hurricane, must talk about everything, and not briefly either. We hardly know

Early photo of Hurricane's quarry operations, when oxen were still the draft animal of preference. This may have been as early as the 1880s. Photo courtesy of HIOBS.

what would become of him if he had to bottle up his eloquence, but luckily he does not have to do so. When he gets so he can't hold in any longer, he hies him straight to Hurricane. There he finds men enough to make quite an audience who are *obliged* to listen to him. He seldom comes on to the island without making one or more speeches. Most of them are of no particular importance, but once in a while he gets to talking in a way that, coming from an agent of the United States government, is so outrageous as to call for indignant comment by all who have any instincts of decency, unless they are bulldozed into silence by the Granite Ring. Of such a nature was his abominable intimidation speech on the eve of the election of 1875; also his bull of excommunication against the *Opinion*, in which he forbade anybody who was at work on the St. Louis government job taking or reading the paper.

Of a like character, from all reports, was the tirade in which he indulged last Saturday, alluded to by our Hurricane correspondent. His scolding, of which his speech was mainly composed, was of no especial consequence, but when he endeavors to bulldoze the men into lying for him, as he did into voting with him, it is time that something was said.

They very properly sent a telegram to Washington informing the department of the substance of Tillson's speech, where it will hardly do that individual any good. He will do well to take advantage of the lesson, and learn that though he may talk bosh, as is his wont, with impunity, there are some things that he had better leave unsaid.

On June 30, 1877, the government ordered work suspended on Hurricane until they received receipted payrolls for that month. The *Opinion* reported: "Tillson waited no longer than the next Tuesday before he came down as gracefully as Davy Crockett's coon, paid off for May, like a little man."

Regardless of whatever Tillson might have believed, Hurricane Island was still a part of the town of Vinalhaven. According to the Vinalhaven town records of February 20, 1875, one agenda item involved choosing a "Committee of three to receive, sort and count votes on Hurricane Island at state elections." On March 12, townspeople "voted to make a District of Hurricane Island and to be named District 12." In November, 1876, the Hurricane Island votes in the presidential election were reported as 130 for the Republicans and 16 for the Democrats. Although there appeared to be at least 146 men eligible to vote on the island in 1876, it was the bitterness over these election results that was at least partly responsible for the labor unrest of 1877.

According to the *Rockland Opinion* which, as usual, jumped into the fray:

> It is hardly possible to account for a vote of 135 Republicans to 6 Democrats thrown by stonecutters, and over one-half of them Irish at that, on the theory of a free ballot. Everybody knows that the great body of stonecutters – and especially Irish stone-cutters – are naturally Democratic; the proportion of Democrats to Republicans among this class is not less than four to one.
>
> The intimidation was not brought to bear to keep men from voting, but to make men vote Republican – many of them having no right to vote at all.

There was a great deal of doubt as to whether the vote could be legally counted. According to a "Letter from Hurricane" published in the *Opinion* on Dec. 1, 1876, there had been a layoff in September of all men who were not citizens. To fill those places, applicants were screened as to whether they could vote in the district and whether that vote was likely to be Republican. It was also reported that men had been discharged from the government (i.e. higher-paying) jobs on Hurricane for reading the pro labor *Rockland Opinion*. The *Opinion* said, "The Governor of Maine and his council ultimately in their wisdom(?) and partisan zeal, preferred to decide, or rather ignore all such questions and count Hurricane in."

In February, 1878, by an act of the Maine State Legislature, Hurricane Island was incorporated as a separate town. "The inhabitants thereof [are] invested with all the powers and privileges, and subject to the duties and liabilities, incident to other towns in this state." The act of the legislature specified that the town "shall be holden to pay all taxes which have been legally assessed upon them by the town of Vinalhaven," and further, that "said town of Hurricane shall be holden to pay one-tenth part of all debts and liabilities now outstanding against said town of Vinalhaven."

A view of the quarry with cut stone in the foreground, in the process of being crated along the edges for shipment. Oxen at upper right date this as an early picture.

Vinalhaven never did get all its money. Either Tillson couldn't, or more likely wouldn't, pay up. Vinalhaven's Town Report of 1879 lists under "resources due from Hurricane, $533.87." Vinalhaven also "Received from Hurricane, $200, in part town debt." But two years later, under Assets, Vinalhaven still reports:

> Hurricane, balance due on Town debt $333.87. The account of the town of Hurricane also remains unsettled, as will be seen by our auditor's report. We have not deemed it advisable to commence a suit against the town to recover the sum due Vinalhaven. The amount is small and litigation expensive, even to the victorious side, and in our judgment should not be resorted to until all other means fail. We would recommend that the town at its annual meeting authorize and instruct the selectmen to make such settlements as shall be just to both parties, and for the best interest of the town.

A similar incident comes to light in 1882, documented by a few sheets of paper in the state archives. Apparently, the Town of Rockland paid out $37.80 to the

Insane Hospital in Augusta for the support of a Mr. Birnie who had been sent there from Hurricane. After some correspondence in the matter, a letter was sent to the overseers of the poor at Hurricane Island:

Gentlemen:

We again send you the bill for the support of William Birnie at the Maine Insane Hospital. Birnie was sent to the Hospital from Hurricane Isle and although he may be a state Pauper it is your duty to see that his bills are paid until the State relieves you of that responsibility.

You will therefore please call the attention of Gen. Tillson to the matter.

Respectfully,

Allen Bowler
Chm Overseers of Poor
Rockland, Me.

A curt reply on Hurricane Granite Company stationery is attached to this letter:

April 3d, 1884

Hon A.F. Crockett

Dear Sir,

We have never heard anything in regard to the pauper matter.

Respectfully,

W. A. Healey

Apparently, Gen. Tillson resisted paying such miscellaneous debts whenever possible.

In February, 1880, an article of quite a different sort appeared in the *Rockland Gazette*, entitled "Hurricane Isle." Why the author chose mid-winter to visit this exposed granite island is anyone's guess. Perhaps, as he suggests, he was stranded. Although why he then stayed two months is open to question. However, what he did in those two months was to write an eyewitness account of the Town of Hurricane. The residents of the settlement were far too busy making history to write it, and so we are fortunate that this unnamed reporter decided to do so. He has given us a window with which to look on Hurricane Island as Davis Tillson's creation before time and the unions had successfully changed his original plan.

The large cutting shed was curved to permit the tracks around the granite works to pass through the center of the building. Stone could be delivered for finishing, then easily loaded and transported to shore. Photo courtesy HIOBS.

Hurricane Isle
"Keep who will the city's alley's
Take the smooth shorn plain –
Give to us the cedar valleys,
Rocks and hills of Maine.
In our North-land wild and woody
Let us still have part.
Rugged muse and mother sturdy
Hold us to thy heart."
Whittier's Lumberman

A daily steamer, the *Hercules*, runs from Rockland to Hurricane Island carrying passengers, freight and mail, and the *Pioneer* makes one or more trips, carrying workmen whose homes are on the other islands; and a small sailing packet sometimes calls here so that the facilities for communication with the mainland are good. In busy times, a small fleet of sloops are engaged in transporting finished stone work in transit by railway.

On reaching the island by steamboat, you are landed on a solid granite wharf, where one large shed is built for storing large quantities of coal, wood etc. Just above the wharf you come to the post-office, a well ordered building, with boxes numbering into the hundreds, and in every way meeting the wants of all. Near this building is Fulton market, liberally supplied with material for the daily wants of the table. A large and well filled store and office of the company stands in close proximity to the post office and market, and then we come to a first-class boarding house, kept by

Group portrait in front of the company store. The boy on the far right and the dog in the foreground apparently had trouble keeping still, and look like spirits. The enterprising mother in the center has made an outfit matching her own, for her child.

Capt. E. Pendleton and superintended by his most estimable lady, where, on the shortest notice, visitors coming on the island have been astonished by the "ever preparedness" of the host and hostess of the house. Here Gen. Tillson makes his home on his short and frequent visits to the works. A number more good houses are kept for the accommodation of boarders, and more than forty small cottages are scattered over the island, and are mostly full to overflowing with men, women and children. We have made but slight acquaintance with the greater number of the dwellers here in their homes, but to a stranger, the dwelling houses on the island look but temporary and slight, yet, inside, he will be happily disappointed and will find more than ordinary taste manifested in chromos, good steel engravings, and fair oil paintings in good frames on the walls; books, magazines and newspapers on the tables; organs, pianos and many other musical instruments scattered about. The omnipresent sewing machine is here; in fact, you will find in these little dwellings more useful, ornamental and tasteful work scattered around on mantels and brackets, giving evidence of a greater average taste among the people, than is found in general society of the same standing. Though outside all may seem hard, sterile and cold, in many rooms into which I am called daily, I find flower stands well filled with rare and valuable plants, and often while the musician's fingers and voices are drawing out the witcheries of sweet tones, the mingled notes of some encaged songster will help swell the strain, and thus render these places home – scenes and "sunny spots," where friends linger and lovingly dwell. In short, I have not, in my large acquaintance with people in the same walks of life, – men of labor and toil – met with an equal number who have apparently the same aggregate of home comfort as is enjoyed by the people with whom I have come in contact.

One great reason for all this is the absence of the great enemy of the working man, "alcoholic liquor." During my stay here of two months duration, and in every day communication with the people, I have not met with a single instance of the use of liquor as a beverage; and I am well aware of the fact that no man can be retained in work here who is even inclined to be "drunkish." The only instance reported during my visit here of the work of liquor happened during the late holidays, and met with a hasty discharge of those who participated; and I know, from the character of the superintendents, that they will not tolerate for a moment this great enemy of the social well-being of working men in their midst; and I can emphatically say, that the people add to their other virtues, temperance, and long may it be ere the rum fiend shall gain a foothold here to blight and wither the prospects of the people on this isolated rock.

In a slight indentation of the island, and on its most prominent point looking seaward east and west, stands the largest and best building; a two story building devoted to public purposes. The largest room on the first floor is devoted to common school and high school purposes, and is capable of accommodating one hundred scholars. It is well heated and well ventilated; the walls not set apart for black-board purposes are well covered with large maps and charts, etc. On the teacher's dais we noticed a large globe, on the table and desk a large quantity of necessary books and other useful material for the teacher's use. I visited this school-room during the Christmas vacation and found it in a remarkably neat, clean and orderly state, and having a large number of skeleton or outline maps, drawn by the scholars during the last term of the school, still on the walls where they pinned them when vacation time came. In the year 1879 the number of scholars was sixty-nine and they had nine months school under the teaching of Mr. Hermon Gilmore of Belfast, a graduate of the State

Normal School, Castine, assisted part of the time by his wife as primary teacher; and their duties were efficiently discharged, and Mr. G. has again commenced his labors for another term. The fact is that a larger amount of money per scholar is appropriated on the island than by any other town or city in the State, being over nine dollars per scholar. Mr. G. has evening school twice a week, which is attended by men and women who are engaged in work during the day, who make choice of this manner of spending their spare evenings in improving their minds, rather than, as we too often find it to be the case among the working classes, in other and less useful pursuits.

And here we must make the remark, that it is owing to the liberal wish of Gen. D. Tillson, carried into active operation, that the advantages of the schools are so great; for he made public statement that he desired them to make as liberal appropriation as they could, and as he pays ninety per cent of the taxes assessed, his wishes have been carried out. We find that the largest amount expended for school purposes in one year was $1077.56. A larger appropriation per scholar is made in this town than in any city or town in the State; perhaps Portland is the next highest. This fact is undisputed.

The next largest room, and opening into the large school room, is used sometimes as a recitation room, and has been used as a singing school room during the winter. On the Sabbath it is used as a Sabbath school room; a good Mason and Hamlin Organ is placed there, and aids much in carrying out the exercises of both schools. In this room during the winter the Sunday evening has been spent by the choir, having a social sing, and a short lecture or talk, as the people term them, followed by a short sing before dismissed. To these reunions all are admitted free, and the subjects spoken upon, have been such as should not conflict with the religious opinions of any who might attend. They have been attended by a fair and gradually increasing audience and no public speaker could ask for more attentive listeners. I should not omit to mention another small room, opening from this room and used as a Library, containing a small but choice collection of books both for the old and young.

The second floor is a large hall, with ante-rooms, and a permanent stage or orchestra, and will accommodate a large audience, and is well adapted for lectures, concerts and other entertainments; and when religious services are held here it is used for that purpose. At present is is used by the Catholics as a chapel for service and as a Sabbath-school room. When the works are full this hall must be a great public benefit.

We must now pay some attention to the works on the island, as from these have sprung all to which we have before referred. The large public boarding houses, six in number, are three stories high, capable of accommodating at least fifty or sixty in each house comfortably, or, in a rush of business, even more than that number, say three hundred and fifty workmen besides the domestics. And, we can speak from experience, they spread tables supplied well with all the substantial and some of the luxuries we sometimes look for and do not find on tables of many so called hotels. The fact is, the people on the island, both at the public and private table, know how to live; and they live well up to their knowledge.

Beginning at the works proper, we look at the quarry, a small mountain of granite with a front face sixty feet in height and some two hundred feet in length with rock awaiting the call; all ready for the steam-drill to sever it from its base and steam cars awaiting to carry it to the different workshops or to the wharf, for railway tracks are laid all over the works and labor, both human and brute, is lessened in every possible

The Shields residence on Hurricane. One of the women in the picture is said to be the first lady to reside on Hurricane Island. The 1900 census lists 19 people in the Shields household, husband, wife, five daughters, a servant, a mother-in-law, and 10 boarders. Photo courtesy Shore Village Museum.

manner. If it should in coming events be necessary suddenly to build up great works, as it may be very possible, here is enough solid material, and here are mechanical appliances of every conceivable character to build up such works, in all their desired massiveness and flank them with a city of tens of thousands of buildings, and leave granite enough for any future calls when the present generation shall have done its work and another shall come to take our places in the ever busy work of life.

We next notice the sheds, as they are called, six in number capable of accommodating fifty men, or three hundred in all, into which, from the quarry, the stone is conveyed for the hammer and chisel of the workman to be applied to it and fashion and fit it for places on our great public buildings in our great western cities; and so minute has been the work in its fittings, that out of the thousands of pieces sent from here but a very few have failed in being placed in their apportioned places.

The blacksmith shops are large and suitable places, containing twenty-four anvils, and are occupied by a stalwart chain of intelligent and sober smiters, (alias smiths) who make their necessary work well appreciated by those depending upon them for the proper carrying out of other labors.

The machine shop is a very neat building overlooking the other works, with trip hammers, metal planers, lathes, and a steam engine of twelve horse power, – forges and every modern appliance for doing it well.

Right at the proper place we find the engine house, with a splendid engine and two boilers of eighty horse power each. I have not the ability, if I had the time, to write of the multitudinous work to which this power is applied.

In close proximity to the engine house is the polishing mill, with its three large lathes, capable of holding columns ten tons weight, revolving with lightning speed under heavy iron planes smoothing their rounded sides – with its carriages of massy beams, pendulums, flexible shafts, and gang saws, all ministering agencies of labor. Many things connected with these works I am not expert enough to understand.

The workshops of this island are prepared to do work second to none in the world. There is a staff of workmen doing ornamental work in granite, that a few years ago would have astonished the world. I have spent some time in my strolls through these works, in the shops more specially devoted to this finished kind of work – work which must be seen to be properly appreciated and which cannot in any manner be described. But we feel sure that this newly developed feature of sculptured and polished granite work, for cemetery and ornamental purposes, is destined to take the place of marble to a great extent, and will supersede it because of the variety, beauty and durability of the granite of the Eastern States.

In the pattern shops we found models and patterns that have been carried out, and are now on the great public buildings of St. Louis and Chicago and other places too numerous to mention, and will remain as monuments of the skill and workmanship of this island long after those toilers shall have gone to rest.

Of the many other shops, such as are necessary to such works, we have not time to write, but we must not omit to mention the office buildings of the draughtsmen and general superintendent, which is like a sentry box overlooking the entire works. Of these officers we shall speak by and by.

There is a good, suitable wharf, down on to which two massive steam cars run, carrying their freight from all parts of the works; and here is a stationary engine which, with the massive crane it works, can take up blocks of work of twenty or more tons weight, and safely deposit them on board vessels laying there to take them to any port of destination.

Of the officers, I wish to say that I have found them at all times gentlemanly, courteous, obliging and kind. In all my communications with them I have found them ready to give me all needed information and advice, and I can truly say that, without fear of being charged with flattery, a finer staff of men I have not met with in public works, either in this country or in Europe.

I would not forget to mention two officers of our general government. Mr. Swandy and Mr. C. Kalloch. They are worthy men, and do credit to the appointments they fill; and as long as such positions may be required may they be filled as worthily as by the present incumbents.

Now the one great question must be in the minds of all knowing these facilities as I do. "What and who has been the great instrumentality in bringing about these events, in the changing of this forbidding isle into the present humming hive of labor?"

To General Davis Tillson who a little more than ten years ago purchased this island, must be attributed the present successful results we have noted, and who has laid the basis of the future prosperity of the works here should he be removed by the accidents of life. Gen Tillson is in himself a living fact, a representative man of his period, a man sprung from the masses with an iron will and determined purpose, not to be easily swayed from his set line, with an extraordinary clear brain, and with vim enough to make a crowd of ordinary men strangers to him, keenly alive to the position he occupies as one born to lead. Underlying these qualities of mind, he has a genial heart, and impulses of a high order. Even those who have most bitterly maligned him, and who like sleuth hounds have pursued with slavering tongues, even those must admit that it would be well for society if we had more like him who, instead of gathering up what he has now invested not only in the works here but in the city of Rockland and elsewhere and retiring into private life, shaking off the very harrassing life he must live in superintending the many works he is engaged in and then seek his own personal ease, as too many are now doing, is constantly purposing some new move that while benefitting, creates labor and scatters means among the many workmen depending on him. And whether in company with statesman, professor, editor, lawyer or priest, he seems ever brimful and ready with some new purpose, awaiting the time for development which, successful or not, shall result in furnishing work for hundreds of laborers and mechanics.

Against such a man it is no wonder that the shafts of envy would be hurled, and that men soulless and inert should seek his hurt. But it will be a dark day should he be taken away, for the toilers will miss him. Long may he be spared.

Life was not always as idyllic as the *Rockland Gazette* article would lead us to believe. For one thing, moving around with large blocks of granite led to accidents. One Peter Toner suffered a freak accident while in charge of a polishing machine. "The car carrying granite to the machine went awry, and pinned him against the wall. He was put aboard the steamer *Hurricane,* and taken to Rockland for treatment." In the *Vinalhaven Echo* of March 29, 1888, we find, "John Patterson met with a severe accident Friday while oiling the engine. He in some manner caught his hand in the piston rod, causing a severe jam to two fingers of the right hand. Dr. Lyford dressed the wound," and on August 2, "P.J. Corcoran, while blocking up a stone in #8 shed, Wednesday, had his ankle badly broken." And in a lighter vein on September 8, "A Vinalhaven girl who is employed in the Hurricane canning factory recently fell through a trap door in the building. The only damage resulting was seriously injuring her new black hose. We state the color of the hose from an eye witness."

CHAPTER TWO

Hurricane's Legacy
Monuments to Posterity

1880–1895

THE REPORTS ALL SEEM TO disagree on the actual number of people on the island. One reason is that the numbers varied according to the work available. In the decade 1875–1885, according to Grindle, there were anywhere from 400 to 1000 men employed on Hurricane. Although in 1880 the Hurricane Granite Company began furnishing stone for the Washington Monument and in 1881, the City of Chicago ordered 5,000 tons of paving blocks, the biggest contracts for the company were awarded a few years later. By the mid-1880's they were hard at work on the Suffolk County (Mass.) Courthouse and the Library of Congress.

One is able to get a view of the life and times of the granite community which appeared regularly in the *Vinalhaven Echo* between late 1887 and early 1889. The brief items, covering not only the ebb and flow of work, but also the social activities on the island, provide more of a day-to-day view of life on Hurricane than the longer, but less regular coverage in the Rockland newspapers.

The years of 1887 and 1888 were also very busy times for the Hurricane Island Granite Company, and few other periods would rival the diversity of the projects on the island which ranged from the cutting and shipping of polished building stone, to the carving of monuments to decorate the country's massive new public buildings and finally to the production of paving stones for the streets of scores of American cities on the Eastern Seaboard.

In December, 1887, the Hurricane column of the *Echo* mentions that carving work on "the group of five angels for the Pittsburgh Post Office" had begun. Four months later in March 1888, capturing the enthusiasm of the times, the paper reported,

> Perhaps the busiest and most crowded corner in Maine, and will be for some time, is Hurricane Island. It may be safely assumed that no town in New England of its size will present a more busy future than this thriving place.
> The Hurricane Granite Company have on hand at present a large amount of granite contracts and there is reason to hope than more will follow. The utilization of the Island's resources have hardly begun, the force at work there now is but a pigmy when placed beside what will be employed there during the present year.

And a month later on April 19, 1888, the prospects seemed even brighter:

> The Granite business is crowded with work . . . a portion of the Library of Congress has been awarded. The Company is spending lots on building roads and laying up wharves. Mr. Reed, superintendant of quarries, is having a large sheet of stone cleared in which he says is stone enough to finish the Boston Court House . . . Garrett Coughlin of Rockland has been engaged by the company to superintend the opening of a new quarry on the island, and work is going on under his direction. That will soon develop a good opening that will supply any demand for granite. Long live and prosper little Hurricane, for its inhabitants are the most pleasant people on earth.

The loading of granite sloops and schooners was frequently reported. For example, on May 24, 1888, "Schooner *Metropolis* discharged a large cargo of freight for the Hurricane Granite Company Saturday and loaded with cut stone for the Suffolk County Court House." Between May 29 and June 7, 1888, three schooners, *Hunter, Mary Brewer* and *Dick William and Son* loaded paving block for New York City. Both the schooner *Eldridge Berry* and the sloop *M.M. Hamilton* sailed during the summer of 1888 for Boston with stone for the new Suffolk County Court House.

The granite fleet of sturdy boats carried cargoes which if not carefully stowed could spell doom to the captain and her crew. The July 19, 1888, *Echo* reported what appears to be a more common mishap when the "Schooner *Clara* of St. John sank off of Little Hurricane. The crew were all saved. The wreck was due to compass error."

Except for the cutting of paving stone which continued on throughout the year in dozens of individual quarries known as "motions," there was a good deal of seasonality to the granite business and the pace of activity usually slowed with the onset of winter when shipping stone was too dangerous and the quarry faces

Facing page: A granite schooner prepares to load up at an island quarry – probably not Hurricane. This vessel is the Frank Seavey *out of Dover, N.H. Photo from the collection of Leland Overlock.*

Below: Paving blocks along the shore road await transport to the streets of New York or Boston or Chicago. Often, these blocks were cut in a "motion" or one-man quarry, by a free-lance stonecutter looking to earn a little extra money. Photo courtesy HIOBS.

Facing page: The Suffolk County Courthouse in Boston, an impressive example of granite block construction, remains in active use among the Beacon Hill government buildings today. The courthouse was built in 1888, at least in part from Hurricane granite.

became icy and slick. On November 8, 1888, the Hurricane Column in the *Echo* reported, "The Hurricane Granite Company are discharging stonecutters. They have (also) let three blacksmith crews go and we understand that there is another to follow." The last report of the year for 1888 on December 12th noted that the "Schooner *Metropolis* of Vinalhaven loads with stone this week."

All of this business activity on Hurricane produced comparable development of the island itself throughout the banner year of 1888. In March of that year, for example, the *Echo* reported "Moses Shields has received lumber and will commence at once to build a barber shop to be occupied by his sons." The same issue noted that "The present year, the Hotel De Pen is to have an extension increasing its capacity to accommodate a larger number of boarders, as the season of 1888 will be one of unusual prosperity. It will have the same genial proprietor of old, and its future capacity will be taxed to accommodate its patrons, as it is at its present size under such pleasant management."

The correspondent also suggested, after observing, "How thick the Italians are," that "the Italian district is much in need of electric lights."

In May, "the diver completed work on the new wharf and left for Boston . . ." and in June, "the Town Hall has been thoroughly renovated and it is now one of the best halls in the county," and then in October, "our new walks and street lamps are a much needed improvement. Mr. Healy has been appointed superintendent of the electric light station."

The column in the *Echo* summed up the year's activities in a column that appeared January 22, 1889:

> It is rather quiet here at present, but the granite business has been very good the past year. The canning factory has done well and furnished employment for quite a number of people. Tenements have been in demand and several houses have been built for rents. A wharf and a large stone shed are being built on the eastern shore of the island. A street lamp is in place on the main street and sidewalks have been built. Although a small town, Hurricane is generally a busy place.

For much of the granite work on Hurricane, stonecutters had to be imported from far and wide; Ireland, Scotland, Italy, Finland and Sweden. It is said that when the foreman needed more workers, he would go to the Italians and get them to write home to the old country to send more men. And they would. Sometimes as many as 30 or so friends and cousins would arrive at Hurricane from a village in Italy. The Yankees were not entirely generous in welcoming them. The "Hurricane Echoes" column of the *Vinalhaven Echo* for May 3, 1888, says, "How thick the Italians are. One lot last week and another expected soon." And on May 10, "Look for another drive of Italians to-night. The woods are full of them." The Vinalhaven newspaper did, however, report that "the nobby suits worn

Interior of the cutting shed (note curvature of track). This photo and the next were in the possession of Beverly Joe Queenin, granddaughter of Onorato Piatti, a stonecutter on the island in the 1890s.

Ornamental carvings in the cutting shed. Photos courtesy of Beverly Joe Queenin.

by the Italians are quite catchy. They are cut on the bias and fulled out all around."

On May 24, a whole article on relations with Hurricane immigrants appeared:

Almost a Tragedy at Hurricane Island

Recently a man somewhat under the influence of liquor, invaded the Italian quarters late at night accompanied by a friend. They demanded an entrance, but it was refused. They made such a disturbance that the Italians came down in a body and attacked the man under the influence of rum, but he got the best of the individual that attacked him and the Italian's wife passed him the axe and he struck the intruder a blow on the head. His friend then drew a revolver and put it against the head of the Italian, threatening him if he struck again he would shoot him on the spot, and thus a tragedy was prevented.

A week later the newspaper reported a small item seemingly referring to this incident. "We understand the Italian contemplates moving to Little Hurricane (an 8 acre island to the west of Hurricane) in order to evade Maine law."

One might well ask how the trespasser was able to become "under the influence of liquor" if this island was dry. Apparently, one of the ships that landed on Hurricane's shore was not there to load granite. Named the *Dark Secret*, she carried a floating bar. Islanders could board the ship and imbibe as well as smuggle supplies ashore. Tillson did finally put an end to this but there were other clandestine sources of supply.

As with any growing town, social activities on Hurricane provided relief, both from the hard physical work for the men in the quarries and from the isolation of the women and children of the island. In March, 1888, the Hurricane column in the *Echo* reported that "a joint stock company has been formed at Hurricane to erect a 'Dancing Pavilion' and they will have the accommodation for excursion parties for the coming season. We wish the boys success."

Later that summer the *Echo* announced that a Hurricane Island baseball team had been formed and had challenged the Vinalhaven team to a game. From the Vinalhaven correspondent of the newspaper the following account:

A five-inning game of baseball, if it could be called baseball, was played here [Vinalhaven] Wednesday this week, between the Hurricane team and the fractured High School Nine that have been mixed up in just such a fix scores of times before. The score at the close of the fifth inning was 11 to 25 in favor of the Hurricanes. The Hurricane pitcher knocked our frightened nine silly at the start and gained a lead that never could be overcome if the Hurricane nine had died on the field. The boys here were so frightened that every time they faced the Hurricane twirler it made the blood curdle in their veins and their hair stand on end as though someone had been telling them ghost stories . . . The club here are going into immediate practice to do the visiting club up when they come again.

Baseball team – Hurricane Island. Considering the fierceness of this team described in the Vinalhaven Echo, the age of the players is surprising. The ages of the team may have varied from year to year. The team name symbolized by "H.A.G." remains a mystery. Photo courtesy HIOBS.

In between dancing, band music and baseball on Hurricane Island, there were outings particularly among the island's management and their families to nearby islands for picnics. A particularly elaborate outing to the White Islands was described in great detail in the *Echo,* no doubt meriting coverage because the attendees included family members from the Landers, Coughlin and White families all of whom were considered fine examples of the island's society. Even routine outings received notice as shown by this item from October 4, 1888: "John T. Landers entertained a party of friends on Green's Island last Sunday. They reported an excellent time with clams, lobsters and milk in abundance." One wonders whether "milk" was a euphemism for something stronger.

As winter approached, with the inevitable slowing of activity in the granite works, the boarding houses also settled back into a quieter routine which no doubt affected the number of young women on the island. The Hurricane correspondent to the Echo reported in November, 1888, "The girls have gone, the Bachelors are organizing a club." A month later the club announced it had 12 members and a club house on Silver Hill. When the school session opened in December with a new assistant, the "Bachelors" submitted the following note to the *Echo,* "We cannot tell yet how [the school] is managed, but think it ought to be a success as the teacher is large enough in both b_____ and m_____." But in January the women had the last laugh, at least metaphorically, in the *Echo,*

View of Tillson's Wharf, ca. 1895, with Mount Desert *steamer docked at right and* Penobscot *pulling in at far right. From the collection of Mabel Kalloch Rollins.*

The second residence built by the Tillsons on the corner of Main and Middle Street (now Talbot) is at the right. A silver plate on the front door said "Tillson," and it had marble fireplaces and crystal chandeliers. It was later purchased by the Rubenstein family, who set up their famous antique business there, visible at left. The Navigator Motel now occupies the site. Courtesy Down East *Magazine.*

"The old maids in speaking of bachelors say they are frozen-out old gardeners in the flower beds of love. As they are useless as weeds, they should be served in the same manner – choked."

By 1880, Tillson was already diversifying his interests. Back in Rockland, he was engaged in his largest and most speculative venture ever, the construction of a great wharf. When he began building the $100,000 promontory in 1876, the people of the city called it a "reckless venture" and predicted certain financial ruin. By the time the venture was finished, the cost had climbed to $200,000. But the General seemed to possess some kind of uncanny insight. The great era of the Maine coastal steamers began in the late 1870's and Tillson's wharf was ready for them in 1881. Up to 30 steamers a day landed there. The *Rockland Opinion* of May 3, 1895, states: " . . . all the steamboats running to this city, with the exception of those of the M.C. railroad connecting with trains at its wharf, make their landings and have their offices [there]. A large amount of other business is also carried on. General Tillson displayed great business sagacity and foresight, as well as commendable public spirit, in carrying through this enterprise. That wharf will always remain a monument to remind the people of Rockland of the work he did here." The *Courier-Gazette* observed, " . . . it proved to be Gen. Tillson's best paying piece of property." The wharf remains to this day, as a Coast Guard Station; the Maine State Ferry Service once there has moved to Lermond's Cove in Rockland north of Tillson's great wharf.

Tillson always found time to be active in the life of the City of Rockland as a member of the Lyceum, a member of the Congregational Church and the Edwin Libby Post, G.A.R. (Grand Army of the Republic.) Having first lived some distance out of town in a house built on family land, he later built an enormous Greek Revival house with an impressive wrought iron fence surrounding it on the corner of Main and Middle (now Talbot) streets just opposite the present-day ferry landing. The house later became well known as the location of Rubenstein's Antiques and was ultimately razed to build the Navigator Motel.

Tillson was not a man to rest on the success of the steamboat trade, however, and in the mid-1880s, he opened a canning factory on Hurricane. The Ocean Packing Company canned lobster, clams and all kinds of fish. Many young women commuted on the ferry from Vinalhaven to the delight of all the bachelors working in the quarries.

The *Echo* reported on April 19, 1888, that Tillson's recently organized packing company "under manager Tilden employs 60 hands a day, putting up 150 bushels a day of clams, lobsters and mackerel." When the steamer *Hurricane* unloaded 130 bushels of clams, the *Echo* reported that the canning factory was "putting up clams in one and two pound cans for the western markets."

Many of the cannery workers came over to Hurricane from Vinalhaven on a local steamer, the *Pioneer*, prompting the *Echo's* Hurricane correspondent to comment that "the Vinalhaven girls that work in the Hurricane factory can be seen together in some obscure spot upon the Pioneer industriously weaving into shape many kinds of fancy work while going to and from their employment."

Looking back over 1888 on Hurricane, Rockland's *Courier-Gazette*, reported:

> The great industry of the island outside the granite business is fish packed by the Hurricane Packing Co., G.E. Tilden, superintendent. The factory last season, commenced the week of April 1, and employed an average force of 50 hands throughout the season, putting up clams, lobster, and herring. The total pack was a little more than a half million cans. The factory shut down Dec. 1st. The business of the company is increasing and more will be done another year. The Company's goods command the best prices and go as far west as San Francisco and down into the southern states.

In 1885, General Tillson and his son-in-law, William S. White, (Jennie's husband), opened up a try works on Green Island for the production of whale oil. Another Vinalhaven newspaper, the *Vinalhaven Wind,* of May 8, 1885, documents a trip over to Green Island to see a freshly caught whale at the works:

The Ocean Packing Company's factory at Hurricane, General Tillson's fish-canning venture. Here, the whole crew assembles outside for a group portrait. The canning factory suffered from the lobster law which limited the size of lobsters which could be taken.

Well, for a person who had never seen a whale before it was a sight worth going a long way to see. We are not so much of a "whale-ologist" but should judge that it was of the species known to naturalists as Physalus Antiquarium, commonly know as the finback. It was, when killed, 67 feet in length, but before it was towed to this place its flukes were cut off, diminishing it by six feet. It yielded about 1200 gallons of oil.

It was killed, we were informed, by firing into it a bomb lance. We have never seen one of these instruments nor heard the method of its use explained. The whale was captured by the steamer *Hurricane* off Monhegan. We next entered the building. In the center were the try kettles, two in number. They are four feet inside diameter and three in depth. Each kettle is composed of two semi-spherical parts, one resting inside the other. The inside one is enough smaller than the other to make a space between the two of about an inch and a quarter. They are bolted together at the rims airtight, and steam is led into the spaces between, thus giving sufficient heat to try out the oil without burning the blubber. This is a new industry for our town, and we hope it will be a successful one. Mr. White, as agent for General Tillson, has leased on Green's Island for three years, a piece of land bordering the inlet known as Sands Cove and has erected three works quite recently. Whales are reported quite plenty on our coast and probably the curious folks will have many opportunities this Summer to see a whale out of water."

Tillson also bought land from the Little Androscoggin Water Power Company and entered a mining venture on Tabor Hill in Vassalboro. And he began going to Florida for the winters. By the end of the 1880's, Tillson became less and less involved in the day-to-day workings of Hurricane. The May 10, 1888, *Vinalhaven Echo* reports, "General Tillson visited the island Tuesday, the first visit since his return from Florida. The General is looking bright and healthy after his winter sojourn. We anticipate many pleasant visits from him during the summer months."

The *Echo* of April 19, 1888, mentions a new firm in the area. "Booth Brothers, the new paving concern that have just opened here, have now at work 35 men, and more are expected immediately. The Booth Brothers are the best known men in the paving business. Vinalhaven welcomes such men to her proud granite-capped hills."

A month later, the *Hurricane Echoes* column reported: "The Hon. William S. White [Tillson's son-in-law was by now mayor of Rockland] visited the island Monday. William Booth and Mr. Donaldson of Booth Brothers were in town Monday night." Apparently, Mr. Booth liked what he saw because in February, 1889, Booth Brothers and Hurricane Island Granite Company merged. The new company included, under one management, quarries at Millstone Point, Conn.; Long Cove (Tenants Harbor), Maine; Atlantic (on Swan's Island); Seal Harbor (Mt. Desert); Hurricane Island; and two quarries on Vinalhaven. At this point, it seems likely that Tillson handed over his part in the business to White, his son-in-law. Although the merger resulted in an impressive corporation, it was a time of many stone quarry closings in Rockland. The report of Tillson's return from Florida in 1888 gives the impression of a man who has made his fortune, built his large house, handed over the business to the next generation and now has the leisure to spend his winters in Florida.

Not so. Tillson had designs on Florida. One Christmas, his foreman in Florida took the time to drop a line to the *Echo* updating townspeople on Tillson's progress there.

Lanier, Florida, December 22, 1887

Friend Healey:

Dear Sir: – I take this opportunity to drop you a few lines to let you know how I am getting along. The climate is very fine and the mercury seldom falls below 60 degrees and just as seldom rises above 80 degrees F.

General Tillson's orange grove looks very well, and though he has shipped 1,500 boxes, he expects to have somewhere in the vicinity of 1,500 more, making a total crop of 3,000 boxes. The General has about 50,000 cabbage plants growing and expects to have them ready for market about the latter part of March and the 1st of April, and the soil is ready to receive 25 bu. of Irish potato seed; he harvested a crop of 30 bu. of sweet potatoes last summer.

The ground is sandy, and I have not seen a stone or rock of any description since I came here. One might imagine he was in tropical America to see the roses in full bloom and tropical plants, fruits and trees growing all around. It is a great country for sportsmen, as game of every description abounds in plenty.

Yours truly,
Rufus A. Coombs

The Florida business continued successfully for almost 10 years until May of 1895. That year, Tillson returned from Florida looking unwell and it turned out that he had been suffering pain in the chest for some weeks. He had attributed it to indigestion and thought little of it. When his condition worsened on his return to Rockland, he summoned the local doctor, Dr. Albert Woodside, who diagnosed the trouble as "an enlargement of the large veins that return the blood to the heart" and very serious. General Tillson made plans to leave for Boston to see a specialist but became too ill to go. Dr. F.S. Knight was summoned from Boston and confirmed the local doctor's diagnosis. The alarming symptoms persisted, and he died shortly before noon on Tuesday, April 30, 1895, at the age of 65 years.

Although the services were very simple out of respect to the wishes of the deceased and the family, and even the sermon was as "brief as the General's former beloved pastor could make it," the entire town of Rockland stopped for the funeral. The *Courier Gazette* of May 7 described the event in detail. The funeral was held in the Tillson house on the corner of Main and Middle Streets attended by members of the light infantry which bore Tillson's name. The description of the flowers alone continues for three paragraphs.

A very beautiful "closed book" lay beside the Grand Army offering, the gift of a number of Gen. Tillson's employees at Hurricane Isle. The body of this book was of white pinks, a stem of magnificent Catherine Mermet roses lying across the page, which

*The tomb of General Davis
Tillson, Achorn Cemetery,
Rockland. Designed by Tillson
himself, with characteristic
foresightedness, everything is
granite, including the fence rails,
and the shingles on the roof.
Photo by Peter Richardson.*

also bore the word "Hurricane" . . . the four employes at the Hurricane Granite Co.s office in this city sending the beautiful roses which were entwined about [the casket's] head . . .

But that which could not have been prevented, and certainly no relative of the deceased would have the heart to attempt it, was the grand outpouring of citizens. Long before the hour of the funeral the family residence, Middle Street and Main, was filled, while hundreds of people in all stages of life thronged the grounds outside, barely speaking above a whisper while the services were in progress. Prominent in this large congregation were the many people who had been given years of employment by Gen. Tillson's numerous enterprises and who had loved him for his many benevolent acts and genial disposition.

This entire funeral procession then processed to Achorn Cemetery where he was laid to rest in a massive granite crypt which Tillson had had the foresight to build a few years before.

Even in death, the true character of the man remained something of an enigma. The obituary in the *Rockland Opinion* states:

General Tillson was essentially a public man, and by his death the public loses a valuable factor in the work of raising the community to a higher level of prosperity and happiness. While he never posed as a philanthropist, and was forced, as we all are, under present social conditions, to engage for himself in the fierce struggle for existence that goes on all around in business and industrial life, his impulses and tendencies were naturally altruistic. If his great mental powers and energies were exerted for his own benefit, it could always be seen that they were also directed and in a measure at least controlled so as to benefit others and promote the general welfare of the community. Those who knew him best, have had the most evidence of this, but it is sufficiently apparent to all who have lived in Rockland during the period of his business activity. It was this disposition and tendency, rather than his unquestionable prominence and influence, that has made his death come to us all with a sense of personal loss; it is that which has caused those who have known him slightly or not at all, or who have been forced by circumstances into antagonism to him, to recognize his worth while living and to feel deep and sincere sorrow at his death.

The *Courier-Gazette*, does not have so many reservations:

General Tillson is dead.
The spirit of a gallant soldier, honored citizen and philanthropist has departed to the great unknown. Just before the hour of noon, Tuesday last, the curtain fell on the last act in life's drama of a man whom the city of Rockland could hardly spare; a man who was a tower of strength in intellect, public-spirited and generous to a fault, a man who could rightly be called a friend to every one deserving of friendship; a thorough christian and perfect gentleman; a man who gave freely of his substance without its being heralded by the blare of trumpets or the beating of drums; and a man who was brave but tender hearted, and who was the personification of truth.

The *Courier Gazette*, a year later, published a list of the major taxpayers in the City of Rockland. The list is several columns long and the highest figure for taxes paid, save one, the Cobb Lime Company, is the "Estate of Davis Tillson – $1,484.63."

Davis Tillson, half-orphaned son of a farmer from the western pastures of the town, had died the richest man in the city.

CHAPTER THREE

Minnie Vinal's Story
The End is Beginning

INTRODUCTION

DAVIS TILLSON ORGANIZED MEN TO turn an island of granite into building blocks for everything from courthouses and custom houses to breakwaters and bridge abutments. The men who worked the granite mound on Hurricane Island took their wives and children with them. These families turned Hurricane into a town rather than just a quarry west of Vinalhaven. In understanding that town, it is important to know what people ate for dinner, how their children were educated, what amused them and how they died.

The story of family life is even more difficult to document than the history of a company which is scattered through union records and newspaper accounts. The story of the families has to be pieced together from more than birth, marriage and death records, census listings and school reports. Most important are the personal recollections of those who lived there. Unfortunately, even the youngest children of the town in its heydey have almost all died by now – 75 years later.

However, because of a high school assignment 25 years ago I started my research on the history of Hurricane Island and met in the process Minnie Vinal (Lyford) Chilles who had spent part of her childhood on Hurricane when the town was booming. The following account of one family's life on Hurricane is based on the recollections of Minnie Chilles.

Facing page: Minnie Vinal (Lyford) Chilles modestly poses for the camera on her porch in Vinalhaven on October 19, 1963. She died in 1965 at the age of 73. Photo by Eleanor Motley (Richardson).

*School children gather for their annual portrait.
One is Minnie Vinal, but which one is uncertain.
Students in the front row have been identified as
Margaret "May" Shields (third from left), her sister
Grace Shields Lambert (seventh from left), and
Helen Patterson Mead (eighth from left). In the
second row are Beatrice Shields Gannon (eighth
from right), and Joseph Shields (fourth from right).
The photo appeared in an article "Life and Death of
an Island" in Down East Magazine in 1957, for
which Minnie was interviewed. Courtesy HIOBS.*

Moving to Hurricane

Minnie Alice Vinal was sitting in the schoolroom on Vinalhaven island on a crisp January morning at the turn of the 20th Century. The room was quiet and the attention of every student was focused on the teacher. In large letters, with her perfect normal school handwriting, she wrote "1900" on the blackboard. In spite of their youth, the scholars felt a sense of awe as the new century had begun.

Minnie never forgot the moment. One reason was that in a few months she and her family were to move away from the familiar Vinalhaven community where she had spent her first eight years. In March, they would go to Hurricane Island. Although one could look across and see Hurricane from Vinalhaven, it was to be another world and one which would leave vivid impressions with her for the rest of her life. In fact, she later gained a certain fame because she could remember living on Hurricane when it was a bustling center of commerce.

Minnie's father, Leonard, was a teamster. He drove horses which by this time had replaced oxen as the draft animals of choice on Hurricane. Leonard was a native Vinalhaven Islander. Minnie's mother was Mary Coyle Vinal who had been born in South LaGrange, Maine. Minnie's parents packed up their belongings and loaded their six children onto the boat. Mary moved slowly for she was expecting again and her seventh child, William, would be born on Hurricane that next August. All were of school age except two-year-old Ruth, and Fred the oldest, who at 18 was already working to help support the family.

Since Mary had her hands full with the children, the growing family would be supported by the combined wages of her husband, $1.25 a day, and her son who as an apprenticed stonecutter would earn 50¢ a day the first year, $1 a day the second and $1.50 the third. The wages, paid once a month, would go into an account at the company store where all life's necessities could be purchased.

Mary faced the change with no little apprehension leaving friends and family for life on a granite rock, a scant 150 acres in size, with a motley population of Yankees, Italians, Swedes, Finns, Irish and Scottish laborers. The life was rough, and masculine, and their small income would have to be very carefully managed to cover food, clothing and rent for her brood.

Leonard's World

Leonard hoped that times would be better than they had been for the past decade on Vinalhaven. The late nineties had been tough going at times as the unions struggled to gain a balance of power with management. The most dramatic event in those years had been "The Great Lockout of 1892."

When Davis Tillson handed over his share of business to his son-in-law William S. White in 1899–1900, the granite business on Hurricane was virtually at a standstill. In 1891, by contrast, there was plenty of work on a $1.5 million contract for a whole block in Philadelphia, the Betz Building, and an order for 33,000 paving blocks for Havana, Cuba. But in the fall of that year, a national depression had begun and the granite business declined along with almost every other enterprise. In 1892, a dispute arose between the unions and management about the time of year for renewal of contracts with laborers. The traditional date of May 1 benefitted the men because the manufacturers had orders waiting to be filled in the spring and workers were in a good bargaining position. Management, on the other hand, wished to change the date to January 1, because then they would be able more accurately to estimate their costs as they signed contracts for the coming year. It would also enable them to cut a better deal because in January the men were hungry and were willing to sign on for less.

Labor refused to agree to the change of date. At that point, a general lockout took place all over New England. Management attempted to bring in "Italian scabs" but the opportunists were put on a boat and their fare paid back to Boston. Hurricane employed somewhere between 350–500 men at the time and it was eight months before a settlement could be reached.

Meanwhile, Leonard and Mary were living on Vinalhaven with their first four children. During the lockout there, a group of stoneworkers got together and formed their own company, the Fox Island Cooperative Granite Company. James Grant managed to procure a contract for 1,500,000 paving blocks from Brooklyn, N.Y. Sidney Winslow, in his "Intimate Views of Vinalhaven" gives the following description of what the granite-workers and their families went through that year:

The Paving Cutters' and Quarrymen's Unions had been practically annihilated by the lockout and the stonecutters were just hanging on "by the skin of their teeth," so Mr. Grant's contracts came as a godsend to the bewildered and jobless workmen.

Local paving cutters and quarrymen began scouring the fields and pastures in search of suitable paving "motions" [one-man quarries]; soon from hillside, glen and forest were heard the musical ring of the tool sharpener's anvil and the metallic click of steel on stone where, for many years previous, nothing had broken the forest stillness but the song of the chickadee, the raucous note of a crow or the pastoral tinkle of a cow bell.

Times were hard and money was scarce; paydays were few and far between; there was a long space of time between the fall of '92 and the spring of '93, during which time the workmen received no pay at all and grocery bills, unpaid, had assumed alarming proportions.

Soon the question came to be asked "When do we get our money for this work we are doing? and as time dragged on the question became more anxious and insistent. The answer was, "Mr. Grant is to arrive in town soon and will bring the money with

THE END IS BEGINNING

him." But weeks and months passed and Mr. Grant failed to appear so the query now considerably more impatient in tone came to, "But when is Mr. Grant coming?" It was a question to which no satisfactory answer could be given, probably not even by Mr. Grant himself and the winter dragged wearily on.

My father was a member of the Fox Island Granite Co., and never will I forget the pall of gloom that hung over our home as the days passed and Mr. Grant failed to arrive.

A view of the village looking north. Note the buildings at the left which are at the top of the hill, including the town hall, and the bandstand. Photo courtesy HIOBS.

Closeup of oxen pulling water on a sledge. About 15 wells supplied water for the whole island, and only a couple of houses were fortunate enough to have wells in the cellar. Hurricaners spent a lot of time transporting water, and dreaming up newer and better ways to transport it. Photo courtesy HIOBS.

But one glad day, just when things appeared to be the blackest, there came the glad tidings, "GRANT HAS COME!" The news flashed over town like a streak of light and "Grant's Come!" was the happy watchword on every tongue, for every citizen was more or less concerned in the man's arrival.

The news was as welcome as the joyful cry of "Cornwallis is taken!" to the weary and war torn Colonists of 1791, and be it recorded to Mr. Grant's credit, he had arrived and with the money to pay off the anxious workmen.

At our school next day the children were all excited and happy and entirely out of hand and it must have been a hard day for the teacher; discipline was out of the question; several times during the day some one of the pupils would raise his hand and announce to the teacher, "Grant's Come!"

Sidney Winslow had a wonderful response to the above article in the *Courier Gazette,* from none other than the famous "Mr. Grant" himself telling what he had had to go through to get that money:

> The chairman of the board got the aldermen [of Brooklyn, N.Y.] to consider our case at a special meeting. Some of us went to that meeting and presented the sufferings, the poverty and plight of the poor Maine workmen. They voted to move from one fund some idle money into the contract fund so we could get our money.
>
> We got that money, and some more from others, enough to help relieve Maine workers. We had difficulty getting coin, which we insisted on getting, from the banks. Why did we insist on coin? That's another story. Jim Murphy and I lugged that mostly gold and silver coin, some in bills, in two grips by train into Maine.
>
> I have never forgotten the scene in that hall in Vinalhaven on that forenoon. The hall was filled with workmen around a large table. We came in, I dumped my gripful of gold 5-dollar pieces onto the table and Jim Murphy did the same with what money he had. Imagine the faces, features and feelings of those men who had struggled and suffered so long and so much.

Life in the Quarries

The lockout had ended on Hurricane in December, 1892, without violence. William S. White, by now manager of Booth Brothers operations in Maine, showed a marked difference in management style from his father-in-law, General Tillson, when he said of the unions that "he much preferred having the men organized."

Hurricane did well in the ensuing years. In 1893, granite was cut for the engine house of the Brooklyn electric light station, a New York dock and a large vault, the jetty at Sabine pass and the Bar Harbor breakwater. In 1894, stone was shipped for the Jersey City Hall and a large vault for Washington Duke of Durham, North Carolina. There were also contracts for the Pennsylvania railroad station in Philadelphia and the extension of the Metropolitan Life Insurance Company building in New York.

In 1895, the end of an era was marked by the deaths of three men: General Davis Tillson, owner and founder of the Hurricane Granite Company; Thomas J. Landers, Hurricane's superintendent for 25 years; and John Booth, a veteran company official. Hurricane's prominent period was over. Hurricane's future financial success would depend on contracts which designated Hurricane granite as the required stock.

From 1895 to 1900, the work on Hurricane had been steady and Leonard Vinal and his family could look forward to some prosperity in the years that followed. Tom Murphy, branch secretary of the Granite Cutters' Union at Hurricane, wrote that conditions in 1903 were "about the busiest I have any recollection of in the granite industry." Leonard had gone to Hurricane really as a last resort. But as the years passed, he did well gaining the respect of his co-workers. When two new unions were formed on the island, the Paving Cutters' Union in 1901, and the Quarryworkers' Union in 1903, Leonard Vinal soon became secretary of the latter. He also served on the town's board of health.

Minnie's oldest brother, Fred, in working to support the family, was doing no more than other boys his age had done for years. The 1887 report of the Bureau and Industrial and Labor Statistics for the state of Maine in 1887, summarizes the "Act to regulate the hours of labor and the employment of women and children" approved on March 17, 1887.

> Section 1. No female minor under eighteen years of age, no male minor under sixteen years of age, and no woman shall be employed in laboring in any manufacturing or mechanical establishment in this state *more than ten hours in any one day* . . . and in no case shall the hours of labor exceed sixty in a week; . . .
>
> Section 5. *No child under twelve years of age* shall be employed in any manufacturing or mechanical establishment in this state . . .
>
> Section 6. No child under fifteen years of age shall be employed in any manufacturing or mechanical establishment in this state *except during vacations* of the public schools unless . . . he has for at least sixteen weeks attended some public or private school, eight weeks of which shall be continuous; . . . "

In 1890, the unions had negotiated for a nine-hour day, eight hours on Saturday. By the time the Vinal family lived there, the hours were 7 a.m. to 4 p.m. on weekdays, and 7 to noon on Saturday. The workers lived to the rhythm of the ringing bell which called them to work in the morning, marked the beginning and end of the noontime lunch hour and told them they could find their way wearily home at night.

The cost of living in Maine *decreased* steadily from 1865 when the Civil War ended until 1887, according to the report of the Commissioner of Industrial and Labor Statistics for 1887. The following list tallies the expenses of a family of six in Rockland for six months in that year:

Meats	$25.35
Fish	11.50
Butter, cheese and eggs	9.83
Fuel	33.69
Flour	11.95
Vegetables and fruit	12.12
Sugar and molasses	5.80
Tea and coffee	3.05
Salt, spices and sundries	19.95
Clothing	33.33
	$166.57

The same report lists the average wages of granite-workers as follows:

Stone cutters	$2.50 per day
Quarrymen	1.75 per day
Sharpeners	2.25 per day
Polishers	1.75 per day
Teamsters	1.75 per day

Interior of the company store. The bunch of bananas is a surprising item to find on a Maine island at the turn of the century – possibly they were sent up by Tillson in his fruit-importing phase. The woodstove in the further room is probably in the Post Office.

Minnie recollected wages in 1900 as somewhat less:

Apprenticed stonecutter	
first year	.50 per day
second year	1.00 per day
third year	1.50 per day
Teamster	1.25 per day
Rigger (for the derricks)	1.60 per day
Laundress	$.30–.40 per load

Prices were proportionate:

Doctor's bill for delivering a baby	$7.50
1 quart of kerosene	.10
1 bar of soap	.07

Since a doctor assisted at the birth of her baby brother, William, in 1900, it doubtless cost her father six days' pay to bring his youngest child into the world.

Life in the Village

When the Vinals landed at the wharf with all their belongings and their six children, they loaded everything they could on a horse-drawn cart which carried their belongings up the hill to their new home. The house, like most of the others, was rented from the company. Few of the workers on Hurricane owned their own homes and those who did had to rent the ground the house sat on. Mary Vinal found herself in a town with a large number of families and children but an even larger number of bachelors. By this time, the ban on strong drink had been lifted on the island and Saturday nights were lively. The introduction of alcohol had necessitated the construction of a lockup in 1895 to accommodate those who got out of hand.

Once the question of lodging had been settled, she turned herself to the next major concern: food for her husband and seven children. Many of her daughter's childhood memories naturally involved food. In good times, they would eat as well on Hurricane as anywhere but in bad times the struggle was severe. Staples were purchased from their small account at the company store. One economical meal that was a great favorite was biscuits smothered in salt pork for the main course or in molasses for dessert. When the store account was low, Mary learned to send the children to dig clams on the north end of the island. Mussels were not commonly used, but you could set a barrel in the ocean to catch lobsters.

In spring, Mary would cut dandelion greens and in the summer her little vegetable garden would begin to produce. No gardens were very extensive as the island was small, the soil was thin and the population was dense. Her relatives would bring apples over from Vinalhaven and the family would string them up to dry in the fall. She had to fetch all their water from a well at the bottom of the hill shared by many of Hurricane's families. If she was late the well would be dry and there was a long wait for the water to seep back in. In 1909, after many complaints from the men, the company began to ship drinking water from Rockland. There were times when hunger was at the door. Mary would send her children out at night to milk other people's cows. Her mother and two sisters came out to visit and the children gathered clams for a chowder. Before the guests arrived, Mary instructed them, "When I call you for lunch, say you've already eaten."

Over the years, most of Hurricane's natural covering of spruce had been cut

Another way to transport water was with a yoke and buckets. This man has a good audience while he balances his load. The horse and cart indicate a later picture than those with oxen.

down. For fuel, the Vinals gathered driftwood along the shore for the stove. But everyone else had the same idea so the supply often was meager. If there wasn't enough driftwood, or it was too wet, a brick soaked in kerosene had to serve. Health was one of Mary's greatest concerns. She had heard the story of the Patterson family where all three children had died of diptheria in one week during February of 1889. The fear of contagion had been so great that the bereft parents had had to bury the children in the night with no one to help. And after the Vinals came to the island, three children of Alexander and Isabella Smith died from tuberculosis. There were drownings and suicides. And the men who worked in the granite sheds were likely to develop "phthisis," a respiratory disease caused by inhaling granite dust.

The reports of the State Board of Health between 1885 and 1905 enumerate the hazards. But compared to other Maine towns of the same period they have little to report. The records for Hurricane show a much lower incidence of infectious diseases, no doubt as a result of its being insulated by 12 miles of ocean.

There was no doctor on Hurricane. Minnie vividly remembered the island's whaleboat kept in its own shed on the waterfront with a pair of skids for easy launching. If an illness or accident were severe, the whaleboat went down the skids and a team of strong men would row to Vinalhaven to fetch Dr. Lyford. He would arrive blue from the cold and scared, too, she remembered, because he knew it had to be something serious if he were called.

Years later, when the town had closed down and Mary Vinal had remained on the island to help as caretaker, her youngest son, William, had an appendicitis attack in the middle of a very cold winter. Born in the summer of 1900 on Hurricane, he was by now about 15. Mary got him in a sloop from Hurricane and set off for Rockland to the hospital. When she got to the far side of the bay the harbor was frozen and they had to finish the journey over the ice with a horse and sled. William managed to survive this ordeal and Mary stayed on with him in Rockland during his convalescence. They never returned to Hurricane.

But that was all in the future. The temptation in looking back is to have events shadowed by what was to come. But in the first decade of the 20th Century there was no reason to believe that Hurricane was not a permanent town. The seeds of its ruin were there: the dependence on one industry, the tradition of company government, rather than self-determination (outside of the union activities), and the lack of private land ownership. Tillson had tried to diversify the economy but the island was very small, lacking room for a busy industry alongside a leisured summer class. The canning factory had been hurt by the new lobster law which as a conservation measure prohibited the harvest of the small lobsters on which the canneries had depended. And even in the granite industry, Hurricane became a fringe operation while Vinalhaven and Stonington were stronger, larger and more durable towns.

"Hurricane Isle, Me., Sept. 30– Oct. 11. The bandstand, the cow, and my sister, Julia Grisson." The note on the back of this photo resembles the note on the one of the Testa house, so this was probably also taken in 1919. The cow had been made famous by a 1916 Boston Post article about the deserted island. Photo courtesy HIOBS.

Entertainment

The people of Hurricane believed there was granite enough to supply many cities for years to come and their position seemed secure. When the week's work was done, the energy for entertainment of all kinds sprang up out of nowhere. The Italians put together a band of mandolins, guitars and concertinas and they would don native costumes and march around the island every Saturday evening with a troupe of children following them, pied-piper style. The Italian band left a lasting impression on the Yankees of Hurricane and other surrounding islands. The Italian music left them "up in the air" as one woman described it while the Yankee tunes "ended at the end." The music of the Italians inspired the Yankees to form a band of their own. The two bands would form ranks at opposite ends of the island and march all over it preserving the smoothness of melodic line despite the roughness underfoot. A bandstand was built and the bands joined forces to compete all over Knox County.

With similar zeal, several pianos and organs were brought over to the island and a teacher from Rockland was hired to tutor 30 or 40 pupils. With the abundance of music and bachelors, it is not surprising that many dances and even a dancing school were organized which people from many other islands came to attend. The Dec. 1, 1887 edition of the Vinalhaven *Echo* advises Hurricane residents, "Dancing school tonight. Don't forget your white shirts, boys." The high point of the year was the "White Duck Ball" to which everyone was invited, adults and children alike, all dressed in white.

Traveling theater troupes did a good itinerant business in the days before their art had been committed to film and Hurricane was definitely on the circuit for one-night, or one-week, stands. A flurry of handbills pasted on every available surface would precede the arrival of the troupe. Old-fashioned melodramas were the order of the day complete with black-mustached villain, beautiful damsel in distress and a hero.

The footlights in the town hall were a row oil lamps with tin reflectors. And there was a large oil lamp overhead. One evening, the Wilson and Clark Dramatic Company was in the midst of a 45-night run on Hurricane. Somebody yelled "fire!" and smoke began to waft into the room. Everybody dashed out. In the excitement, Jim Hayes got his head stuck between the rungs of a chair and had to be sawed free. Soon people realized that it was a false alarm. Some damp wood had been put into the furnace. They filed back to their seats and the show resumed. When all was quiet again, a voice was heard calling, "Help! Help!" On looking around they discovered that Barney McNulty had climbed out the window in the excitement and had hung there by his hands the whole time waiting for rescue.

Once even a motion picture was brought to Hurricane. Minnie remembered,

"Women not given to weeping cried like children at that picture. I was thrilled and cried myself, but I was uneasy, too, for I'd never seen my mother cry before, even about real-life trouble."

For Minnie's brothers, baseball was the sport of preference and there were plenty of strong young contenders for the team. The girls, too, formed a baseball nine which practiced "on every nice afternoon" but there is no record of their playing other towns. One wonders how, after a full week's work of hauling granite around, the quarrymen entertained themselves with more physical exertion. But perhaps a baseball seemed a light load after all those tons of rock. The men's team played Vinalhaven often and traveled around to other harbors and the mainland to compete. In doing so, they risked the caprices of the weather. Sidney Winslow of Vinalhaven gives an eyewitness account of 135 players and spectators from Vinalhaven on such a tour who were fog-bound and had to spend the night on the boat without food or water.

The older men played a game called "roller ball" introduced by the Italians. It was played on an "alley" of packed ashes. The ball, about 4 inches in diameter, was rolled down the alley and the idea was to make it stop on a target at the far end much like shuffleboard. Hurricane also had its own bowling alley and pool room which made for an indoor sport during inclement weather. The Italians formed the Italian Socialist Club and the Italian Dramatic Club with the proceeds from their performances going toward the renovation of the Town Hall. Another option for entertainment was to take the Saturday night boat to Rockland where the bordellos lined the waterfront.

Religion

Tillson had originally made provisions for interdenominational services of religion on Hurricane which met upstairs in the Town Hall on Sunday evenings. He even took the money for their support out of the men's pay, raising some objections. But soon the ever-increasing Catholic population started having services of their own. In 1900, the Archdiocese of Portland decided to build a "mission church" there, the only church to be built on Hurricane, which was under the protection of St. David's Church in Rockland. It was nearly completed in 1901 when President McKinley was assassinated. The first service held there was in his memory. A priest came to the church once a month. Non-Catholics were excluded only from communion and confirmation. One island resident went home to Italy for a visit and brought back the church's proudest possession, a small white cabinet for the altar, blessed by the Pope.

A rare exception to the land ownership policy was made in the case of the church. In 1908, Tillson's daughters, Jennie White of Rockland and Monira Day of Dubuque, Iowa, deeded the plot of land around the existing church, sixty-eight feet square, for "one dollar and other considerations" to the Bishop of Portland. This ownership was granted with the stipulation that the Diocese of Portland maintain the land and building "in suitable condition" and hold regular services there. If the Diocese should fail for a period of five years to hold regular services, the land would revert to the Tillson heirs. Thus, in subsequent real estate transactions, the clause "with the exception of the Catholic Church and lot" appeared

Left: The Catholic Church, Hurricane Island. The cross on top was gilded with real gold, and the windows were stained glass, with the names of the donors on them. An anteroom at the back was for the use of the priest for storage and preparation for the service. The land on which the church sat was owned by the Bishop of Portland.

Facing page: The organ was one of several items which was brought to the Catholic Church in North Haven when the church closed on Hurricane. It is still there, gathering dust in the mellow light of the North Haven choir loft. Photo by Eleanor Richardson.

on two deeds to Hurricane until the statute of limitations finally ran out. The summer community on North Haven Island decided to build its first Catholic church on that island in 1910 and years later after the abandonment of Hurricane Island, they were happy to integrate the Hurricane church pews, organ and altar into their edifice. The chalice which had been donated to the Hurricane Church by the Shields family was also brought to North Haven where it resided undisturbed in an unlocked church for 62 years until it was stolen in 1980.

Written on the back of this photo is "Hurricane Island. This is Mrs. Shields who lived near the Town Hall and the school house. Such a nice lady!" She was doubtless the mother of Dorothy Shields, Minnie Vinal's best friend, and Minnie probably came to this house often to play.

Minnie's World

While Minnie Vinal was aware of the hardships and struggles of her parents, and could describe adult life on Hurricane in later years, she was still a child in 1900, following pursuits of children everywhere. She had plenty of playmates starting with her six brothers and sisters. Beyond the family circle there were 62 other children in her new school. Fifteen of these were within a year of her age. They were mostly born in this country but their parents had a wide variety of backgrounds. The number of Italian children of school age was minimal in 1900 although there were 61 Italians on the island.

Of these, Minnie soon befriended Nellie Keay and Pearl Dushane with whom she never lost touch in later years. But it was Dorothy Shields who became her lifelong friend. They saw each other often, long after they both had left the island.

In 1880, Hurricane spent more per pupil on their school than any other town in the state. The Maine School Report for 1880 lists per pupil expenditure at $9.97. The next-highest town is Muscle Ridge, paying $2.89. The total budget was $798 for a 40-week school year. Although the teachers were mostly male at first, they soon were replaced by female teachers. All were graduates of normal school. The women's wages decreased steadily from $8/week in 1884, to $7/week in 1886 to $6/week in 1890. This may have been partly due to the general decrease in the cost of everything starting with the end of the Civil War. But when male teachers did come, for brief periods, they were always paid more.

Twenty years later when Minnie arrived in 1900, there were two teachers for the 63 students, one who taught the winter term, and one who taught the summer term. Neither one had attended normal school. They were paid $11.50 per week (5 days), and the town paid $3.50 for their board. Weeks of instruction had shrunk from 40 to 33. Attendance averaged only 50%. Per pupil expenditure was still higher than average but no longer the highest in the state. Annual school expenditure was down to $588.

Despite the discouraging statistics, Minnie had very positive memories of those teachers. "That teacher was part genius and part missionary. She could teach any subject to students ranging in age from five to eighteen," she recalled. Minnie was amazed to find that many of them could not even speak English. But with the mutual cooperation of students and teacher, most managed to get a good education. The older ones helped the younger ones. They learned mainly reading, writing, figuring, geography, algebra and bookkeeping. The language barrier presented a real problem for many of the new little citizens. One Italian child was simply called "Little Mary Bald Island" because no one could figure out how to pronouce or spell her name.

If the Italian children were behind in the classroom, they became the teachers outside of it opening up a wide world of new customs to Minnie. Forever cheerful and happy despite the drastic change from sunny Italy to the frostbitten Maine coast, the Italians gave a bright touch to everything. They built gazebos for the brief warmth of July. They wore bright clothes dressing up in native costumes with red and yellow sashes on Saturday nights. They ate different food, spaghetti and Italian bread, and shocked the Yankees by giving wine to their children. But if Minnie was amazed by some of the Italian customs, she was greatly impressed by their artistic talent. In addition to their music, their granite sculpture was unexcelled and they frescoed the ceilings of their plain little New England houses after the fashion of their ancestors. A woman once asked one of the sculptors how he managed to chisel a magnificent stone eagle out of a block of granite. The sculptor replied, "Oh, there's really nothing to it, Ma'am, for you see the eagle was already in the stone and all I had to do was chisel it out."

Minnie and her friends had the run of an island full of sounds and excitement. Not only music, but clicking hammers and groaning machinery pounded away all day long. Their schoolroom was not far from the quarry where huge chunks of stone were continually being drilled and blasted. Blasting happened about once an hour during the day and once every two minutes after 4:00 p.m. when it was certain that everyone was out of the way. The air was often filled with sticks and stones.

The children were part of all that went on spending long hours on the shore watching the granite boats come in. They were able to identify them all by name. The majority were large sloops about 85' x 25' with only about seven feet draft. The sails were made extra heavy to pull the weight of the granite. For loading, a derrick was rigged to the mast. The sloops sailed mostly to Boston where the granite was loaded onto railcars. But sometimes they sailed as far as New York or Washington. They had names like *Tarrantine, Margaret Ford, William Booth, William Bisbee, Harvester, Brigadier* and *Yankee Girl.*

The children's leisure was not guaranteed. Child labor was a fact of life and Minnie's older brother, Fred, was not the only teenager helping to support his family. Child labor was a hot issue at the time. A law was passed in 1907, forbidding work days of more than 10 hours for girls under 18 and boys under 16. However, the labor unions on Hurricane had by this time ensured that no union member would work more than eight hours per day.

The children of Hurricane experienced the whole spectrum of life there – the battle for survival, the times of joy and celebration and the times when the battle was lost. Minnie described a night when two Finns, out in a boat in the thick fog with with too much rum, drowned within hearing distance of the shocked islanders. And when one of the boarding house residents fell head-first out a window onto the hard granite, either intentionally or unintentionally, she observed, "We all ran up to see his brains." Suicide Rock, in the center of the island,

was so named because a Swede climbed up on it one day, made an impassioned speech in Swedish, then drew a razor and cut his throat.

Minnie was not sheltered for long in childhood. At her mother's knee, she learned to knit ear tips for her father's horses to keep the flies off. At thirteen, she left Hurricane to live with her grandmother on Vinalhaven and work in the horse net factory there. At sixteen, she went to work in the post office where she worked fairly steadily until her marriage at twenty-one. She married Dr. Walter F. Lyford, the nephew of the doctor whom she had seen come over many times in the whaleboat for emergencies. They had two children, Walter in 1915 and Ruth in 1922. Dr. Lyford died in 1927 of Bright's disease at age 51. Minnie was left a 35-year-old widow with two young children. On December 18, 1928, she married

"Master Tommie Landers became the proud owner of the first carriage and pony for riding in November 1890," says the Rockland Courier Gazette. *Tommie was the son of superintendent John Landers. Perhaps Tommie and his pony found a sled for winter use. Photo courtesy HIOBS.*

"Rockside Cottage, Hurricane Island, July, 1907." Note the hammock in the yard, and the elaborate shed system leading to the privy. Photo from the collection of the Vinalhaven Historical Society.

again, this time to John Chilles. Their daughter, Mary, was born in 1929 and lives on Vinalhaven still, now Mary Olson who follows her mother's career of postal work. Minnie lived on Vinalhaven for the rest of her life. Her second husband died in 1952 at age sixty-two. Minnie continued to share her Hurricane memories with many people until her death in 1965. Minnie Vinal Lyford Chilles was one of the last who remembered.

The End of an Era

As Minnie was busy growing up and away from her family on Hurricane, the life was slowly ebbing out of the island's granite business. Beginning around 1905, architectural styles began to change; new materials, notably concrete, were developed and costs of cutting and shipping granite rose along with the cost of everything across the nation. Hurricane enjoyed a brief respite in 1909 when a contract for the St. Louis Post Office was awarded. A new shed was built and a new compressor purchased. But the death struggle had begun. In 1910, General Tillson's family bought back the business from Booth Bros., and the Hurricane Isle Quarries Company was organized. The president was Tillson's son-in-law, W.S. White. The treasurer was his grandson, W.T. White, and his daughters, Jennie White, and Monira Day, were directors.

In 1912, despite a contract for granite for the Bar Harbor breakwater, the report from Hurricane to the Granite Cutters Journal was, "It looks like another close down unless the company gets something else soon." One factor that kept them going was their skillful and tenacious superintendent, John T. Landers. Landers had grown up on Hurricane, the son of the superintendent, until he left to attend Rockland Commercial College. He was one of the youngest, at 14, ever to complete the course. He followed that with technical studies in Montreal and a course at the Massachusetts Institute of Technology. He then returned to Hurricane, starting out as a draftsman, and ultimately succeeding his father as superintendent of the works. He was retained by the Tillson heirs when the change of management in 1910 occurred. At this time, the quarries were leased for two years by the Coast and Lakes Contracting Company, which kept him on as superintendent of works. Landers was also a selectman of the town of Hurricane for nearly 25 years having been elected to that position almost as soon as he came of age.

In 1914, hopes rose once again with a contract for 1,200 tons of granite for the breakwater in Rockport, Mass. Landers supervised the cutting of the stone over the summer and the loading onto a stone scow in November. The following account from the Rockland *Courier Gazette* of Nov. 10, 1914, tells the fate of Hurricane's last shipment:

Almost a Tragedy

Captain Ansel A. Philbrook of Vinalhaven and a seaman named Henry Tonette were near to death in Rockland harbor Sunday morning, when stone skow No. 63, owned by the Coast & Lake Cooperative Co., foundered.

The craft was in tow of the Boston tug *Pallas*, which was not aware of the distress signals until the hawser had been cast off and the tug had started for her berth. She immediately went alongside and the two men were rescued from their perilous position. Half an hour later the scow was at the bottom of the harbor, securely pinned by her cargo of granite, which weighed between 1100 and 1200 tons.

We left Rockland at 1:30 Sunday afternoon, said Capt. Philbrook, bound from Hurricane for Rockport, Mass. When we were within about three miles from Monhegan we encountered a heavy southeast gale, which was kicking up a heavy sea. We did not think it safe to continue so the tug *Pallas* turned back toward Rockland.

The sea broke over the scow constantly, and by the time we had rounded Owl's Head, seven of the ten pockets were nearly full of water. The pumps were kept steadily at work, but could make no headway.

We sounded the whistle repeatedly, and shouted at the top of our voices, but the sound was not heard on board the tug until the hawser had been cast off. By the time she had come alongside, the scow was half under water.

It is reported that the craft is not insured.

Ansel Philbrook, the scow's captain, was the father of six children at the time. The scow sank on November 8, 1914.

Sixteen days later, by a strange turn of fate, the stalwart superintendent John T. Landers died in Rockland of typhoid fever. He was only 46 years old. The final blow to the town of Hurricane was not so much the sinking of the ship as the death of this one man. In the minds of company officials, there was no one to take his place. The next morning the drilling and blasting stopped, the great engines of the polishing plant were silenced and never again was the work whistle to blow on Hurricane Island. The people were gathered together and told that work would be permanently suspended. The order was so sudden that most of them had only enough money put by to get themselves to the mainland to find work. Furniture was left where it was, pictures remained on the walls and the tables were left set for the next meal. Hundreds caught the boat out in the next few days and Hurricane was left in suspended animation like the last days of Pompeii. For years residents of Vinalhaven or other nearby islands who visited Hurricane would vividly recall the eery feeling of seeing evidence of the island having been abandoned almost overnight. Tools were literally laid down in place on faces of granite that were actively being worked when the last whistle blew. Tools in the process of being forged were laid on blacksmith anvils. Cutting sheds were full of partly finished blocks that were being cut to final shape. And Company houses, full of personal belongings, remained intact on the hillside overlooking the wharves. Hurricane Island became a ghost town, but the ghosts seemed eerily present around the once mighty granite works of the island's cliffs and in the shadows of the scores of houses huddled together on the stark hillside on the eastern shores of this company town.

With the sudden death of the enormously talented John T. Landers, who, together with his father, Thomas Landers, had managed the day to day activities of the island's granite business for the past 44 years, it is no exaggeration to say that the town made from granite also died.

Only a few remained to look after the island. Among them were Mary Vinal and her youngest son, William, and John Landers, uncle of the superintendent, who had come to work the quarries in 1872 as a boy of 19 and saw no reason to leave after 42 years. The old-time powderman, John Fleming, who was covered with scars from his run-ins from "Old John Henry Dynamite" and a cow named Bessie also stayed. John Landers told a *Boston Post* reporter two years later:

> Ain't it a pity. All these nice houses with no one living in them. And to think that a few years ago we were having our little times together, our marriages and funerals and christenings, all the little things that go to make up a real, happy life. But we'll have them again. Concrete is all right in its way, but they're goin' to come back to the good old granite, and don't you forget it! Hope the old crowd comes back then, those who are still alive. I like it here, but it gets kind of lonesome at times; lonesome for the old faces, you know.

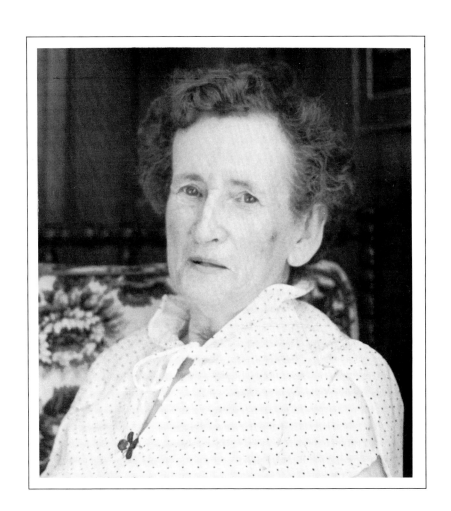

CHAPTER FOUR

Margaret Philbrook's Story
Childhood in a Ghost Town

INTRODUCTION

IN MARCH, 1988, 25 YEARS after the interview with Minnie Chilles, I once again drove to Rockland and took the ferry to Vinalhaven in search of information on Hurricane. Sharon Philbrook, the town clerk, had told me she had the vital records which I had thought were lost. But it was her advice to visit her Aunt Margaret in Eliot, Maine, which proved to be the greatest discovery.

Margaret Philbrook (Kossuth) Smith is 75 now and was one of the last children to grow up in the town of Hurricane, if you could call it a town, since when she lived there the island was full of empty buildings.

Seventeen years after Minnie Vinal came to live at Hurricane, Margaret and her family set out from Vinalhaven for a new life on the island. Margaret was one of nine children – soon to be ten. Her father was Ansel Philbrook, captain of the ill-fated scow that had carried the last shipment of granite from Hurricane, the scow that sank in Rockland Harbor. He and his wife, Nellie, had agreed to be caretakers in a town with no people. They would be responsible for looking after the place and ultimately for tearing down all the buildings to be sold for lumber.

Margaret has such a remarkable memory that her amazingly clear recollections of Hurricane's history preserve one more view of the island's history.

Facing page: Margaret Philbrook Smith in September, 1988. Despite certain physical disabilities, Margaret is totally self-reliant, with a powerful zest for living. Photo by Peter Richardson.

"The Philbrook children take great delight in getting out the old desks that were once in the schools on the island. On the left is Margaret Philbrook, while seated is her brother Willard," says the Boston Post, *July 30, 1922.*

Margaret's Story

I don't know how my father got the caretaker job on Hurricane, but when the superintendent died and the island went down in 1914, a lot of people moved off the very next day. They left everything – tables all set just as they was laid out. There was nothing for them to do but to go get a job somewhere else. I suppose my father had moved off the island then because I wasn't born there. He went to Vinalhaven. And I was born on Vinalhaven in 1913.

I think it was 1917 when we went out there. I remember my father packing up the town records and shipping them off to Augusta. That's when we first went to Hurricane. I don't remember what the box looked like. It could have been a wooden box, because they used wood a lot in those days. It didn't cost anything to ship anything hardly either. A few pennies.

When we got there the man that owned the island was McDougall – from Rockland. He only owned it a short time when he sold it. I'm not sure that he got any money for it but William S. White owed him some money or something and they traded. And then William White owned the island from then on. Mr. White used to have hunting dogs. He used to board them with my mother on Hurricane. So we always had all kinds of dogs to play with.

The Philbrook Family

My mother was born Nellie Raymond on Vinalhaven in 1885. My father, Ansel Philbrook, was born on North Haven in 1878. They lived on North Haven for a long time when they was first married. I think one of my brothers was born on North Haven in fact, two of them might have been – Charles and Ernest – I can't seem to remember where them two was born. But I know they must have had to live there before I was born because that's where they came from when they moved down to Hurricane. North Haven doesn't have a granite rock on it but Vinalhaven's full of rocks. North Haven's got just about enough to make a few stone walls.

My father and mother had lived out there on Hurricane before with their family – with the children that was born before I was born. My oldest brother Charles went to school on Hurricane, and he had to have been just a little boy then. He must have started school there. He was born in 1905. I'm not sure whether Ernest did or not, I can't remember. Never heard of him going but he was the next in line, but I know that Charlie went because he had his Hurricane report card. He became Captain Charles Philbrook. He ran the Vinalhaven boat to Rockland for a long while. Willard, another brother, was just two years older than I was. We used to pal around together, Willard and I.

We had one brother that was born on Hurricane while the island was running. His name was Pearl R. Philbrook. He was born in 1912 just the year before I was born, April the 25th. Right after the *Titanic* sank. He lives in Springfield, Massachusetts now. I don't know why they named him Pearl. I guess our mother must have just liked the name Pearl or something. During the war he had trouble. They'd draft him and tell him where to go. And he'd get down there and they'd be all women. It was a woman's name, Pearl. He said three times they got him down there, then they'd send him back home again. So he never did go to war.

I had a sister, Dorothy. And I have a brother, Lyford, that was born after me when we lived on Vinalhaven. Lyford was named after the doctor that brought us all into the world. That would be young Dr. Lyford, Minnie Vinal's husband. And then they moved back to Hurricane and Father was caretaker there. We lived there seven years. We moved out there when I was between four and five years old. I was born in 1913. Our baby brother, Albert, was born on Hurricane on June 17, 1920. We have another sister that was born years after. She lives over in Portsmouth. Annie was born after we'd all grown up. Dr. Shields delivered her.

Going to School

All of the time we were there, Hurricane was a plantation form of government. When Hurricane became part of Vinalhaven, they changed the name of Vinalhaven at the same time. The Haven used to be a capital "H." And then they made all one word out of it. Three or four years, we didn't go to school at all because the state was dickering how or whether they was going to put a teacher on there to teach us children. Six of us that would have gone to school. But you had to have seven to make it compulsorary for them to put a teacher on there. So then they decided that our father would have to take us to Vinalhaven. But he wasn't going to take us unless he was going to get paid for it. So they gave him $2 a day for landing us on Vinalhaven. And he used to land us at the shore in the Thoroughfare next to Green Island. And then we walked two miles to school and two back. He'd come and get us at night.

He had a sloop boat. It had a sail on it but usually he used the engine. And when it rained he'd take us way down to Carver's Harbor. And we'd walk from there. And then if it come up a storm, late in the fall, we'd go just as long as we dared to. My sister Dot got seasick every time. She never did get used to it. We had to stay over on Vinalhaven sometimes. We'd go along the road with our brothers and knock on the doors and ask the people if they'd take us in. The boys always found places for Dot and me first.

Sometimes we had to stay in the boat. As you look across Hurricane to Vinalhaven there's a place called Old Harbor. My father used to get up as far as there sometimes – it'd be an awful storm – and he'd drop anchor and we'd ride it out all night. And our mother used to say – I've heard her tell it so many times – she said she almost went crazy. She'd look out, you know, and she'd just see the end of the mast because it was rocking so. She was afraid we'd all get drowned before we ever got across. We laid there all night lots of times. So we went for seven years back and forth to Vinalhaven that way. But just in the spring and fall. Our older brothers taught us in the winter. We played school just about every day. We had the old school desks from the island and the school things in the top of the barn.

The Philbrooks on Hurricane, July, 1922. Front row (from left) Margaret, 9; Pearl, 10; Willard, 11; Dorothy, 8; Lyford, 5. Back row, Smith, 12; William, 14; Ansel Philbrook; Albert, 3 (born on Hurricane); Ernest, 15; and Charles, 17. Mother declined to have her photo taken. From the Boston Post, *July 30, 1922.*

The Buildings

We lived in a house down near the island's steamboat landing. That big old barn was between our house and the road before you got to the cove. We walked up the hill a little ways to a well for our water. We were supposed to tear all those buildings down. Some people owned their buildings, but not too many. They were mostly all company houses. The ones that owned them, some of them wanted to tear them down and save the lumber and make a house somewhere else. Mr. White owned most of them. He'd sell a whole house, that's the way he'd do it, because when we tore them down, we tore them down in such a way that the lumber was all saved. The windows even. Everything was saved. And then, we used to put the lumber and everything down to the wharf and someone who bought it would come with boats and get it. Then they'd either build it somewhere else or make whatever they wanted out of it. A lot of houses have got Hurricane lumber in them.

I had eight brothers, six older and two younger. Me and my sister helped tear the buildings down, too. In the summer and the winter we tore down buildings. And we'd slide the chimney bricks down to the wharf on our sleds during the winter.

One time my brothers, Ernest and William, took it into their heads to go around the island pushing over outhouses. Our father was in one.

I used to wear a sailor hat all the time. They couldn't keep that hat off me. And I was frozen all the time. I never got warm. It was my system, I guess. I had to have clothes, coats, long stockings and everything. Well, it's about 15 degrees colder than Vinalhaven. You get a rake of the wind right down through Hurricane Sound.

The name of the wharf was called the loading wharf. That's where they used to load all of the granite. It's to the north of where the steamboat landed. But it's almost the same wharf. It goes the whole length of the shore. There's a jog that makes a separate wharf, the loading wharf.

When you came straight up the hill from the steamboat wharf, the church was on your left. I don't think the church was moved to North Haven like you've heard. And I don't remember a Protestant church. Just the Catholic one. It had three beautiful leaded stained glass windows on each side. They each had a picture of a saint, or something, and on the bottom was a square with the name of the person who donated it. I went back once, after I grew up and we moved. I went back two or three times but the last time was in 1939, I guess. And the door was down then, and instead of going up the steps, people was walking on that door and going in. But someone had broken in and stole the carpet. There was no carpet on the floor any more. But the Catholic people came and took all the artifacts and things out of there. They went to Rockland, I think. Over in the

Looking toward Green's Island from Hurricane Isle, a coastal schooner prepares to load granite. Collections of the Farnsworth Museum, Rockland.

Catholic church. So as far as them moving the church, I never heard of them moving the church.

You know, I can't seem to remember what became of the town hall or where it even set. Unless it was called – they didn't say that it was a socialist hall did they? Because they had a lot of people on there that was, what do you call them – socialists or something? Yup, and that was their hall. The Italians built it. They used it for all kinds of things. I don't know how they could have moved it. It was up off Broadway. Or you could get there if you turned right after the schoolhouse at the top of the hill and walked down toward Broadway. It was in behind the houses.

The town hall could have been in the top of the school, but I don't remember it ever being up in the top of the school. The schoolhouse was a great big building all by itself. Do you know the old steamboat landing? Well, you go right straight up from there, that was a road at one time, and there was a sidewalk on the left. You went part way up the hill and turned right after the McCormack house and that was Broadway. But if you didn't turn, and you went up to the top of the hill, on your right there was a great big building and that was the school house. We tore that down and Roy Coombs bought it. He hired us to help him tear it down. I remember we pulled nails forever. I don't think he put the building up somewhere else but he used the lumber for something. Right beyond the school was what we called Ol' Lady Landers' house. It had the most beautiful apple tree in the yard – with sweet russet apples.

Did you ever hear of Broadway? It was nothing but one big ledge. It was beautiful, all white. It was white just like you'd scrubbed it. There were four or five houses on one side. There was two houses, the McCormack house on the right and the Shields house on the left. Then there was a space. You could keep on going up Broadway and there was four or five more houses. And then as you got up to the end of it there was three or four nice big houses up there.

We used to get a lot of snow in those winters. It was up to the cross bars of the

Postcard of a house in the village with children in the roadway. This may have been the superintendent's house. The Testa house is marked with an arrow in the top right corner of the picture.

telephone poles. It would come a hard crust. And we would climb up on top of the snow and we would slide down the snowbank and that's how we would get into a lot of them houses. The snow would go to the bottom of the windows. Then we would go up on that snow and climb in through the windows. But believe you me, we covered our tracks so our father wouldn't know we'd been in there. Our father wouldn't allow us to go in the houses. Kid-fashion, the minute he was gone for one day off the island, why we'd go and have the greatest time going in the houses. But the doors was all locked, you see, and we couldn't get in, but sometimes there'd be a square of glass out and we were small enough that we could squeeze through that square of glass.

September 1919, the Testa house. The Testas continued to come out to Hurricane during the summers after everyone but the Philbrooks had left. Vinchanso Testa was a lobsterman, having been employed earlier in the quarries. The house is gone, but the pole for birdhouse remains.

The furniture and everything was all in them. And the table was set just like they'd walked right away. In those days, you know, when they'd get up from the table and the women would do the dishes and put everything away, they'd set the table for the next meal. And, of course, there was tablecloths on every table. They never ate off a bare table. There was no plastic, of course. There was oilcloth and cloth.

Vin Testa lived way up at the end of Broadway, the last house up, and there's a high bluff rock there. His house was built right in under it and it had a bird house on a pole. And underneath that rock was a ledge about as long as the house was and they had a piazza thing. There was no roof over it. It was like a big step. You come out and stepped down once and it was all rock and then that rock went right up. And it was clean. You could sweep it all out and dirt and nothing ever got in there. You come out of the door and come down around the end of the house to come back to Broadway. They had a hen house right there, and a hen yard. The Testas lived in Rockland. They used to come only in the summertime. He was a lobster fisherman. And then there was Mr. and Mrs. Benner that used to live there. He went lobstering, too. And Johnny Shields and his sister, Mary, would come out for two or three weeks in the summer to the Shields house on Broadway. And he'd go in the church and play the organ by the hour. My brother Willard and I would go sit in the pews and listen just as long as he'd play. I remember the bandstand, too, and my mother told us about them playing at that bandstand. There was an Italian band and an American band.

Down at the southern end of the island is Barsugli's Cove, and down there was Barsugli's boarding house, next to Barge's Head. There was another one set right next to it that was called the Block. And another next to that and that was Nichols'. Then across the way was the Patterson's boarding house. Then down beyond that there was another one. But as I remember, it was nothing but a cellar hole then. That may have been a place for the men to wash up when they come in from the quarry and took off their dirty workclothes. A kind of bath house. I don't know what the name of that one was. So there were five big boarding houses. The water would come almost right up to where they were built.

We used to have a lot of fun in them old boarding houses. We used to play all kinds of games in them. There were stoves, great big black iron stoves that burned wood. And they had a door on both sides. And you could crawl right through them. So we used to hide in there. We used to play hide and go seek. They had what they called a smoke room. In the evening, that's where the men-folks used to gather. There was a big old pot-bellied stove in there. But I don't think the big rooms where they slept had any heat in them at all.

In the smaller houses they had just the woodstove in the kitchen. Up in the top of the ceiling they'd have a thing they called a register. That was all the heat they had in the bedrooms. They must have had to bring a lot of the wood onto the island. The big old boats with firewood used to come to Vinalhaven, even. They used to burn everything in those days, even spruce. That's why they had so many fires.

Down on the western side was a great big building. It was a double tenement up in that little cove. That was Tom Sullivan's and Jerry Sullivan's. They were two brothers with their families. One lived in one half of the house and one lived in the other. Tom was the postmaster. Jerry drove the grocery wagon.

As you came up from the wharf was a big, drab building. That was the store and in the front corner, that was the post office. They had a big platform that was right across the end of the whole building. And they walked up on that and put their letters in the slot. They used to put money in if you didn't have a stamp. So when we tore that building down we got a lot of money out of that corner where it slipped through the crack. There might still be some there. The old Indian heads and the old "V" nickels had a Liberty on one side and a big "V" on the back instead of a buffalo. And there were some nickels with a big "5" on them. And right across from that store was a bowling alley. My mother used to keep one of them big old, bowling pins at the top of the stairs as a weapon when my father was away with the older boys and she was at home with the younger ones. One night my brother, Charlie, came home late. He'd got some new white gloves he hadn't told her about. When he put his hand around the door, she thought it was a prowler and he almost got it with the bowling pin.

Entertaining Ourselves

With ten children, we didn't have any trouble finding things to do. In the winter time we played with our sleds and things. They were homemade, too. Mostly, we'd slide down Broadway because that was almost a glare of ice. We had the whole run of the island. We had beautiful places to play.

But I'll tell you what we used to do, I don't know if anybody in the world ever did it, but some apple trees on there had real beautiful apples. But they were so old that they didn't have too many apples on them. They wouldn't have a barrel on the whole tree. But we gathered up all there was. Each one of us kids would take a box and we would go into the woods someplace and dig a hole and bury them, way, way down where the frost couldn't get to them come wintertime. Then in the springtime, when our apples in the barrels that our father had bought was getting low, we'd go and dig up our apples. And we'd trade them with our brothers to get something they had.

If you went by the school house at the top of the hill and kept on going on a little bit of a slope, and you went for about, oh, maybe a quarter of a mile along there, on the left was the pond. We had our play boats on the pond. Our brothers

*The younger Philbrook children
enjoyed a whole fleet of large
model boats built by their father
and older brothers, the boats all
had alarm-clock motors. The
"lockup" is visible at upper left.
Photo courtesy of Margaret
Philbrook Smith.*

and father made us the boats. We had an awful lot of them. And we had engines in them all. They were made from old clockworks .

The little quarry hole is the one we used to play in the most, even more than the pond. Not the quarry in the valley, but the little one next the big quarry. There was only one place that was real deep. The big quarry had trout in it. When we tore down those boarding houses, they had wooden sinks in them. Father gave them to us kids. We stopped up the hole and they were our boats. We had canvas over the bottom and we painted them with three or four coats of paint. And then they were waterproof. They were big, five or six feet long by three feet wide. And there was two, I think, in every one of them boarding houses. That's what we paddled around in. Our mother used to let us go down and play in them any time we wanted to.

People came out the year round while we were on the island. You'd be apt to see anybody anytime. Then there used to be a lot of those big yachts come down from North Haven, the Herzogs and people like that. There was no vandalism or anything. There was some people who came back and got their furniture. My mother bought some furniture out of some different houses. I don't remember what become of the rest of it. Maybe thrown away. Maybe they gave it away.

We used to play at J.T. Landers house, across from the church. One time my mother went down to the barn in the summertime to pull some shingles out of the pile to build a fire. A big old frame was sitting on top of the pile of shingles. So I went down, kid-fashion, and I got to playing with that frame. And my mother said to leave that alone or you'll have that down on your head. Of course, I kept right on, kid-fashion. And bye and bye, it fell down, and there was a nail in it. It hit her right on her head. I was scairt to death. I thought she was going to give me a licking. So I ran out of there as fast as I could, and I ran up to Landers' house. They had a great big horse chestnut tree up there. And I went up that horse chest-nut tree. I stayed there until dark because I was afraid she was going to give me a licking. I think I gave away about every toy that I owned to my brothers and my sister if they would just play around that tree so I wouldn't be up there all alone. Well, it came almost dark and my mother came up and says, "Well, you can come down now." So I come down. But I didn't get no licking. I don't think she ever licked us once.

You know, I've thought so many times, if it had been me on that island with ten kids, I would have been crazy. All them little kids running all over that island, they could have got drowned in those quarry holes. I don't know if she ever worried about us. But she must have. My brother Willard and I used to chum around together. And then Dot and Pearl was together a lot. We all played together. But if we went anyplace around the island it was always Willard and I that would go. So every morning at five o'clock, Willard and I'd get up, winter and summer, and go all the way around that island to see what had come ashore in the night. We

could have slipped overboard with all of the ice in the dead of the winter.

We used to find a lot of weir poles. You probably don't know what a weir pole is. Well, they used to make weirs to catch herring in the coves. And these poles would come up out of the mud. They'd get loose and drift off and they'd have to replace them. They were nice poles and you could get quite a lot of money for them. Maybe a dollar. That was a lot of money in those days. So we earned quite a lot of money by getting those. We bought a lot of our school clothes with the money.

My big brother, Smith, got a new hatchet one winter and he wanted all of us little kids to see him cut down a tree. That tree was frozen and bent down in the snow. When he hit it, up came the tree and broke his nose.

Then we used to have what we called a sling-shot. We all had one. We used to make ours out of the crotch of a tree. Then we'd take an old piece of rubber that was down around the works and tie it on. And then we'd take the tongue of our shoes for the thing to put the rock in. But we didn't have rocks too much. We had what you call the ends of plug drills. They'd drill a hole in the stone with a plug drill. They get dull and after a while they'd break off and they'd throw them away. Then they'd make a new end. When you hammer it, it comes down like a chisel. Then you hammer it once, then you have to turn it, then hammer it again and that makes the hole. That was all hand work. And when the hole was deep enough, they'd put two little things in there. Then they'd put a wedge down the middle and they'd hit that and that would break the stone along the grain of the rock. If you didn't go with the grain you'd break it and lose your stone. It wouldn't be no good.

We shot birds – them little sea birds – with our slingshots. We could hit them things as quick as could be. And then we'd take them home and cook them. We used to call them Jenny No-Tails. They were just about as big as a pigeon. They were winter birds. We'd have to fish them out of the water after we'd killed them. We'd take a pole or something and try to get them ashore. I don't know why we didn't fall overboard.

Survival

Besides birds, we ate a lot of fish, I know that. We caught them. Lobsters were always around the wharf. You could fish them up with a fish line. You could see them down there. You'd keep the hook going up and down until bye and bye it would catch on something and you'd pull the lobster up. There was much more lobsters then. Mother used to tell when she was little she'd go down on the shore and just pick them up. Doesn't seem possible. That would have been the early 1890's.

We used to eat a lot of salt fish. Salt fish was good. Our father had a business of salt fish while he lived there. He used to buy fish and salt them in big old hogsheads. Then he sold them. Codfish, hake. You had to freshen it out. I love salt fish. You soak it in water and let it come to a boil. Then change the water, then boil it again, then taste a little piece of it to see if it's freshened out enough. You still want some salt left in it. Making salt fish, first you catch the fish and split them down through the middle, then lay them out flat. Some people put them in pickle. But usually they plaster the salt all over them, rub it right in, and then put them out in the sun to dry and then turn 'em over to dry the other side. It takes three, four or five days to dry one fish. They get hard, not awfully hard, because they're too thick and there's too much salt in them. And that's a salt fish. And you don't have to refrigerate them.

Mother made two quarts of flour into biscuits three times a day. That's how much her sifter held. The thing we liked the best. We used to have it for supper on Sunday nights usually. We'd fry up some salt pork and put some molasses in your plate, put some salt pork fat in that and sop the biscuits in that. That was good. You could sprinkle the salt pork pieces over the top. You ate any kind of vegetable you could get. We had a garden. But our father used to buy a lot of vegetables. And he used to buy barrels of apples and eight barrels of flour every year, white flour. They used to buy sugar by the barrel in those days. I don't remember maple syrup, just molasses. We didn't have too many sweets. I suppose there was so many of us my mother couldn't make too many sweets. She used make a great big one-layer cake. We used to love that. And she used to make johnny cake, like corn muffins only there isn't quite so much leavening in it. It's a little bit harder. It has a little bit of sugar like corn bread.

We loved mussels. We had lots of mussels and clams. There was one place when the tide would go out extra long up on the northern end of Hurricane that you could dig clams. You go by the valley and by the little quarry. And as you go north around the end, when there was an extra low tide. That's where we found them.

We had hens, a cow and a horse and a pig. There were berries, lots of raspberries. Not too many blueberries. We used to go across to Green's Island to get blueberries. And we used to go over there and get a lot of apples. There's a lot of nice apple trees on Hurricane, too. There was some blackberries and a lot of huckleberries, like blueberries, but on a high bush and black. And there were lots of wild strawberries. We could go over to Vinalhaven and get food. Our father went once a month in the winter to get supplies. They had so many things laid in that there wasn't too many things except the staples that you might have to get. We had milk from our cow and eggs from our chickens.

Sometimes we got sick. Once, all ten of us children caught the measles at the same time. Our mother's pig caught them, too. She doctored him along with the

rest of us and he lived. My brother, Lyford, whatever he was playing with, he put it up his nose. One day he was helping my mother cut up beans so he put them up his nose and couldn't get them out. They tried everything, a button hook, a crochet hook. Finally they had to go over to the doctor in Vinalhaven to get the beans out.

The winter that Hurricane Sound froze over we were on the island five days with nothing to eat. And Albert was a baby. Our father was going to kill the cow the next day if they couldn't get across to get any food at Vinalhaven. Well, they didn't get to Vinalhaven. Instead they took the town dory from the boathouse on the shore, and went to Heron Neck Light on Green's Island and they telephoned the order from there to Vinalhaven. The steamboat, when it came our way from Carver's Harbor on Vinalhaven, was supposed to stop when he could see Hurricane. Then the boys and my father was to row that dory over to the steamboat to get our groceries. But, it was all froze over. What father and the boys had to do was get out on the ice and they'd pull the boat and then they'd get back in because the ice would break, and then they'd push with the oars until they'd get to another big ice cake. Then they'd get out and pull the boat again.

But the steamboat never stopped. It kept right on going. So the next day when the ice had kind of broke up they got to Heron Neck Light again. They telephoned again and the captain said that he would see to it that they stopped. So they went out the next day and they got the groceries off the steamboat that day – the same way – pulling the dory over the ice.

Us ten kids were all howling we were so hungry. Our mother sent the oldest boys around in the houses to see if they could find anything that the people had left that we could eat. Do you know what a firkin is? Well, they found one of those full of brown stuff that looked like graham flour. Mother had plenty of fat left from when they killed the pig, so she mixed that flour up with some of the milk from the cow and made doughnuts out of it. And we ate it. But we didn't know if it would kill us or not. Nobody knew what it was. We named it "Rough on Rats." That was a survival, all right. But father didn't have to kill the cow. They got across on the fifth day. Of course since Albert was a baby, he needed the milk from the cow. So they held off just as long as they dared. But they was going to kill it the next day.

Life After Hurricane

We left the island because it was sold. So my father was no longer the caretaker. Anyway, we'd torn down most all the houses. My father and brothers went back a couple more winters to take down the rest. They moved to Vinalhaven and I finished out school there. I only went through the second year of high school.

*Wedding photo
of Margaret Philbrook Smith's
parents, Ansel and Nellie
Philbrook. In later years, Nellie
refused to have her picture taken
because bearing ten children did
away with her girlish figure.
Photo courtesy of Margaret
Philbrook Smith.*

View of the main cove at Hurricane with the town whaleboat in the foreground. This is the boat which was sent for the doctor in Vinalhaven in emergencies, and the one used by the Philbrooks in their desperate trip for food one winter. Photo courtesy of the Farnsworth Museum.

Then I went out to work. I did housework around a lot of different houses doing piecework and housework, day work, or whatever you call it. Then I went to work for a summer hotel that was on Vinalhaven. And then I went from there to work for the Gastons who owned Hurricane Island. It was in 1939 that I went to work for William Gaston. He had owned Crotch Island for a long time. He bought Hurricane Island in 1936 when the bank that owned it closed in receivership. He was Jimmy Gaston's father. Jimmy's the one that owns Hurricane now. He's a doctor in New York. He graduated from the big hospital up in Montreal. The Outward Bound School leases the island from him. And then there's Billy, he's the older boy, older than Jimmy. I think he owns Spectacle Island. Billy came to see me last fall and he was telling me about camping out there on Spectacle Island. But he only goes there in the summertime. He works in Washington, but he lives in New Jersey. Tommy, he's the third brother, owns Crotch Island.

I went out to Crotch Island to cook for Mr. Gaston in 1939 and then in the fall I went back to Connecticut with them. They came from Brookline, the Gastons did. But William lived out in New Canaan, Connecticut. So I brought the three kids up for nine years. I had one month off during the summer.

I worked for him until 1944. Then I got married the first time. My husband was from Vinalhaven. His name was Bill Kossuth. We bought a farm on the road going from Rockland to Camden. It's where the Pen-Bay Medical Center is now. We lived there on that farm for a couple of years. But my husband took sick. He'd gotten arsenic poisoning in the Aleutians during the war and he got cancer. We finally went back to work for the Gastons and my husband died there in 1949. I stayed with the Gastons for two or three more years. Then I went to work at Harmon Hall School in York, Maine, a private school. I met my second husband there, Bernard Smith. He and I were married in 1951.

Then Bernard got a job chauffeuring for Mary Kearny in Princeton, New Jersey. We moved to Washington, D. C. with her. I'd cook for her in a little kitchenette in the Wardman Park Hotel. We'd go to Florida and New Orleans every winter. We worked for her for 14 years, and when she died, we stayed on another year to clean the place out.

We were married 29 years. Bernard died in 1980. How time flies.

CHAPTER FIVE

Hurricane Island Outward Bound School
The New Era

THE HURRICANE ISLAND OUTWARD BOUND School opened in 1964, just 50 years after the overnight exodus of Hurricane's granite-people.

The purpose of the school is " . . . to conduct safe adventure-based courses structured to inspire self-esteem, self-reliance, concern for others and care for the environment."

In 1988, I visited Hurricane Island with my husband, Peter, to see the island in its present-day incarnation as the focal point for a program which now has 17 bases from Maine to Florida with an enrollment of 6,700 men and women.

George N. ("Buz") Tripp, our Hurricane Island Outward Bound School (HIOBS) contact, met us at the school's headquarters in Rockland at 8:30 on an August morning with a green backpack in one hand and a large, black photograph album in the other.

We climbed down a long ladder onto a freshly-painted motor vessel named *Reliance* and set out into pea-soup fog for the trip across Penobscot Bay. The captain, Chris Wells, had his face in a radar mask most of the way and told us that for the majority of trips that summer he had been navigating only with radar.

Facing page: The quarry's seamed cliff is an excellent training ground for the Outward Bound School's climbing course. Climbing is carefully supervised for safety. Photo by Eleanor Richardson.

Buz Tripp demonstrates the scale of this massive block, which is typical of those which had to be moved about the island. They still are strewn about the old quarry. The row of drill holes on the face is characteristic of granite cut by the plug-and-wedge method. Photo by Eleanor Richardson.

Buz Tripp is the school's unofficial historian. Over the years he has become the self-appointed guardian of a sizeable collection of old photos. The collection was started by Betty Willauer, wife of the school's founder Peter Willauer, in the 1960s and augmented by longtime staff member Eliza Cocroft-Bailey and others. Buz has also attempted to locate and to exhume as many landmarks of the old town as possible, awakening an interest in the island's story among Hurricane Island's new residents – students and staff alike.

Our arrival at the island was abrupt. We saw no other islands after leaving Rockland, nothing at all but fog, until two boats materialized at misty moorings – and then we were at the pier. This was Valley Cove where most of the school's landing and leaving takes place. The pier was small but solid, built for loading granite.

We turned left and walked along the shore on a crushed granite roadway past HIOBS' big boat house built near the site of the old whaleboat house, and the slip which Ansel Philbrook had used to launch the town dory on his desperate trips after groceries the winter of the big freeze.

"Now down on your left, above the pier is our main building and dining hall. It sits on the foundation of the old company store," Buz pointed out. "And across the road is the bank – there are two safes in the cellar. We've recently liberated the foundation from the spruces." We left some of our gear in the main building and turned right up the hill beside the old reservoir.

Water was so very precious on the island that they tried to conserve every drop. Buz pointed out an old spring lined with round sea stones at the upper end of

The flywheel of the steam-driven air compressor from which hoses ran to the top of the quarry to power the rock drills. The flywheel, which is over six feet in diameter, is said to have been the largest flywheel ever cast when it was installed by Tillson. Photo by Rick Perry.

Left: Steam was generated in large boilers, and piped around the works wherever it was needed. This steam-drill replaced the old hand-drill method, and speeded up work (and noise) considerably. This drill stands on the main wharf at Hurricane today, and another from Hurricane may be seen at the Maine State Museum in Augusta. Photo by Peter Richardson.

Facing page: Granite is cut by splitting along the grain. First, a hole is drilled, then two plugs are dropped into it. A "plug wedge" is inserted between them and hit with a hammer to split the rock. When the works closed down, many of the plug wedges were left right where they were. Photo by Peter Richardson.

the reservoir. "We've found fifteen wells on the island with an elaborate system of cisterns and culverts, but this is the only spring. I've read about ships stopping here for water even before the town was built, so I would guess this is that original spring," he said. In fact, I had read a story about two old sea captains who were in the habit of stopping by Hurricane for water. One was Captain Cain. As they limped up the hill on their old sea legs, his companion urged him on, "Hurry up, Cain," and that's how the island, according to one account, was supposed to have gotten its name.

Continuing up the road by the reservoir, we came to the churchyard on the left whose posts were more elaborately carved than the other simple, square fence-posts on the island. A graceful "1900" was etched on one. The church foundation had been painstakingly cleared and a simple stone altar erected. "We've had several christenings here, and one wedding," Buz informed us. Across the street was a square of plain granite fenceposts, and two giant trees, one an elm and one a horse chestnut. Surely, that was Margaret's tree, the horse-chestnut, where she'd hidden from her mother.

As we reached the summit, Buz pointed out a foundation on our right that was much larger than all the others. "This has got to be the town hall/school building," he said. "And across the street beyond it, this L-shaped foundation is the house with a picket fence in the middle of the old postcards." A flight of granite steps led into the deep cellar of a large house which boasted its own well with a neat granite cap. We later learned that this was the Landers house where two genera-tions of the family that had supervised the granite works had lived. Buz took spe-cial pride in two recently liberated lilac bushes in the front yard. A small circular pile of stones under one of them showed a former garden decoration. Meanwhile, my husband busied himself photographing old medicine bottles which had been dug out of the foundation and a rusting metal bedstead.

From the Landers house, we descended the western slope by the ice pond where the Philbrook children had played with their toy boats. It is now used for "initiative" problem-solving exercises. Large orange floating devices dotted the shore. And a cluster of exotic pond-lilies grew undisturbed on one side. We descended into the large meadow beyond, with two little man-made ponds at the bottom, designed, no doubt, to catch the overflow of water from the upper pond and conserve it. We agreed that this meadow was a likely spot for the baseball diamond. It was handy to the boarding houses, now reduced to four immense foundations on the slope toward Barsugli's Cove. While one lay in tall weeds, the others were full of trees and considerable bushwhacking was necessary to walk their borders.

When we reached the water, we came to an elegant house of glass and natural wood tones nestled on the edge of the cove belonging to the island's owner, Jim Gaston. Turning left down the path among the spruces toward the big quarry, and

The church was built in 1900, as this gatepost testifies. The first service was a memorial service for President McKinley, after his assassination. Photo by Eleanor Richardson.

The "pulling boat," a trademark of Hurricane Outward Bound School, is a common sight in the Fox Islands. Here, a Hurricane crew sails up the western shore of North Haven Island. Photo by Peter Richardson.

A climber must fall to catch a rope, in order to reach the next stage in his ascent. The previous climber waited twenty minutes to get up her courage. Photo by Peter Richardson.

gazing out over the grey stones across to Barge Head shrouded in mist, I was struck by what a really beautiful place this island is. We couldn't resist pausing from time to time for a handful of the lush raspberries which grew everywhere. Coming around the quarry, the cliff face suddenly came into view. Three climbers were splayed across its face and a few people had gathered on the opposite shore to watch them. The first climber sat at the top belaying his comrade below with a long rope. The second, a young woman, had just spent many minutes in the middle of the rockface getting up the nerve to jump for a swinging rope that must be caught to get to the next stage of the climb. The third stood in the middle of the cliff with his toes hooked in a granite seam. Custom has it on Hurricane that when this point is reached the climber has to sing a song. His voice echoed to us across the quarry with a lusty rendition of "O Tannenbaum" in German.

We risked being late for lunch, so we hurried back around the end of the island to the dining hall. People gathered together and joined hands for a moment of silence before diving into the hearty vegetarian repast which was spread before us: marinated seaweed, hummus on homemade whole wheat bread, salad and brown rice with vegetarian brown gravy.

Peter volunteered to go back along the shore to photograph the details of stone and machinery along the wharves and the quarry while I wanted to see the graveyard on the north end of the island.

We paused along the way to see three high foundations in a row with a well in front of them which just two years before had been invisible in the woods. The Outward Bound crew had gone to work and now there was a charming clearing. The connection between those foundations and the three "stone-cutters' houses" in one of the old pictures was obvious. As we neared the north end of the island (passing the one sandy beach where the clams could be dug), we came upon two unusual foundations. They were notable because the stones were round seastones gathered from the shore rather than the crisply cut blocks of the stone-cutters' houses. "I think this must be the oldest foundation on the island," said Buz, "The one that pre-dates the granite settlement." We examined the cellar hole and nearby well. "This larger foundation may have been a barn or it may have been a pen for keeping animals," he guessed. "I'm told that this big mound over here in the woods is the grave of an ox. I imagine it would take a lot of digging in this thin soil to bury an ox any deeper." It was hard to tear oneself away from this mystical little one-house settlement and easy to fall into speculation about what life must have been like for the lone settler and perhaps his family on this northern shore.

It was a few steps farther to the tiny cemetery. Just two stones bore testimony to those who had died over the years on Hurricane. One was elaborately carved in Scandinavian lettering, and said simply "Erik" on one side. The back identified him as Erik Lawson, aged one year, seven months, and twenty days. He was the son of Alex and Paulina Lawson.

The other grave belonged to William Webster, aged 52, who had died on Sept. 12, 1902.

We walked around on the soft spruce needles for several minutes searching for the hardness of other fallen stones under the surface. But there were none. Buz's copy of the 1910 map showed about fifteen graves in the graveyard and he was concerned that over the years the graveyard might have been vandalized.

Another theory which had been offered by one of the mates on the Vinalhaven ferry was that some of the graves had been moved after the island closed down. They might have been taken to Vinalhaven, or Stonington. Margaret Philbrook Smith says that there was never a large cemetery there when she was growing up but that everyone buried their dead on their own land whether they owned it or not. She said there were two or three graves here and there in several yards, such as the Pattersons' whose children had died of diptheria in 1889. For now, the mystery of that foggy graveyard remains to be solved.

It was time to stop searching and make our way back along the shore to the boat. Buz, at one point stood in the mist waiting for me to catch up and reached into a nearby spruce to touch a piece of hanging grey-green lichen. "This is really like a northern rain forest," he observed. And indeed, every spruce looked as though it was decked out in grayish, misty, Christmas decorations, the moss hanging everywhere. "Old man's beard, they call it," he said.

We headed back toward the boat – and civilization. There was so much to try to capture in that short time, so much we wanted to remember later. We caught the boat at four, amidst a cheery bunch of inner-city kids, boys and girls, on a day trip from the new program at Thompson's Island in Boston. Our boat pulled away from the misty shore, and I realized our day on Hurricane was over. In true Maine fashion, the sun maddeningly chose this time to come out in all its glory and spread its warmth over the bay as Hurricane became a smaller and smaller shadow in the boat's disappearing wake.

Appendix

THE LISTING OF DESTINATIONS FOR HURRICANE granite is fairly self-explanatory. Granite buildings are massive and many probably still exist. One cannot fail to be impressed, for example, coming upon the Suffolk County Courthouse when wandering about the backside of Beacon Hill in Boston. One marvels at the vast amount of stone in the building. This list has been culled from various sources, mainly newspaper items and from Grindle's Tombstones and Paving Blocks.

The Vital Records are listed here as an aid to those searching out their family history and as a tribute to all those who lived, worked, struggled, succeeded and failed on the island over the years.

The vital records date from 1892 when the state of Maine first required that they be reported to Augusta. There is a reference in one entry to the "old book," indicating earlier records, but that book seems to have disappeared.

Spellings are variable. Not only did Yankee town clerks and census takers have a lot of trouble with Italian and other names (the people reporting often did not speak

English), but even the same name was spelled in various ways. In the record of births, for example, Katharine Shields, who bore six children, has her first name spelled five different ways. Some names were anglicized, i.e. from Nectora to Nichols. In addition to those problems, the handwriting is often very difficult to read.

BIRTHS – Some earlier births on Hurricane may be verified by looking at the parents' place of birth in the birth, marriage and death records. The youngest child of Ansel and Nellie Philbrook, Albert, was born on Hurricane when the family was living there as caretakers but is not listed. He was born on June 17, 1920, the last child to be born on Hurricane until Rachel Parker was born on Hurricane on June 11, 1972, the third child of Rafe E.A. and Catherine Bird Parker. Dr. Ralph Earl from Vinalhaven assisted at the birth in school director Peter Willauer's cabin, the only one with running water at the time.

MARRIAGES – The record of marriages will help unscramble some of the name changes of the women on the island. The marriage dates indicate who married whom, as space does not permit listing them side by side.

DEATHS – The record of deaths, when read closely, tells many stories: the young man who, widowed at the age of 35, committed suicide with a razor; the statistics of Erik Lawson and William Webster, who lie in the graveyard at the northern end of the island. And most poignantly, Adline Smith. Adline's mother died when she was 15. At 19, Adline bore the child of an unknown father and she herself died soon afterward of a heart problem. She had named the child Isabella after her mother. When Isabella was 1 year and 7 months old, she died of "Tuberculosis Meningitis." The death record says she was born on Hurricane, but she is not listed in the record of births. Her mother is listed as Adline Smith, and father is "unknown."

CENSUS – A lengthy census is available for 1880, 1900 and 1910. The 1890 census was unfortunately destroyed in a fire (before the days of multiple copies). A Xerox copy of these is available from the author, P.O. Box 1843, Andover, MA 01810. (Please send $5 to cover Xeroxing and postage.) The population of the island in 1880 is recorded as 220, in 1900 as 257, and in 1910 as 256. This may not have taken into account the five boardinghouses with 50 men in each.

This piece of finished stonework is ready to be loaded on the unique rail cart Tillson designed to carry both rough stone to the cutting sheds and finished stone to the loading wharf for shipping. Photo courtesy of HIOBS.

Partial Listing of Hurricane Granite Destinations

1877   St. Louis Post Office
        St. Louis Customs House
        Fall River, Mass., Post Office
        Chicago polished columns and pilasters
        Brooklyn Bridge, New York
1878   Monument in memory of Confederate General Sterling Price – St. Louis
1879   Monument in memory of Rev. Andrew Barnes, former pastor of the Rockland Parish
1880   40,000 cubic feet of granite for the Washington Monument
1881   5,000 tons of paving for Chicago
1882   Granite for the basement of Baltimore Post Office
1883   Approaches to the north wing of the State, War and Navy Building in Washington, D.C.

The Suffolk County Court-house in Boston, an impressive example of granite block construction, is still a busy place today. The front entrance and facade are typical of the massive public buildings of the time. The courthouse was built in 1888, in part from Hurricane granite.

1884   Lubec, Maine channel jetty
      New York Central Depot extension
1885   Pittsburgh Post Office extension
1886   Library of Congress, Washington, D.C.
1888   Suffolk County Courthouse, Boston, Mass.
      Paving for New York and Boston streets
1889   Fall River, Mass., Courthouse
1891   Betz block in Philadelphia
      Unity Building in Chicago
      33,000 paving blocks for Havana, Cuba
1893   Brooklyn electric light station
      Bar Harbor breakwater
      Sabine Pass jetty
      New York dock and a large vault
1894   Jersey City Hall basement
      (Burial) vault – Washington Duke of Durham, N. Carolina
      columns for Pennsylvania Railroad Station , Philadelphia
      extension of Metropolitan Life Insurance Co., of New York
1895   Colonel Brown residence, New York City
      Baltimore Court House
1896   Onandago County Savings Bank, Syracuse, N.Y.
      Presbyterian Church, Philadelphia – polished front
1898   Girard Estate (?)
      Buffalo bank
1899   Bridge over Mill Creek, Thomaston, Maine
1901   Metropolitan Bank Building, New York City
1902   Fidelity Trust Building (?)
      Two buildings at U.S. Naval Academy, Annapolis, Md.
1903   New York Custom House
1905   Chemical Bank of New York – columns
1909   St. Louis Post Office
      New railroad terminal of Chicago and Northwestern Railroad,
      Chicago – bases of columns
1912   Bar Harbor breakwater

Stone from other quarries finished at Hurricane

Museum of Fine Arts, Boston
Cleveland Post Office
Silsbee Tomb – New York
Buffalo bank

Finished stonework still sat in elegant solitude at the site of the former cutting sheds at the south end of Hurricane Island 50 years after operations ceased. Photo by Eleanor Motley Richardson, 1963.

Hurricane Island Record of Births 1892–1915

Date	Name	Sex	Last Name	Father	Mother's Maiden Name	Father's Birthplace	Mother's Birthplace
1-17-92		F	Wasgatt	George	Annie Hasson	Cherryfield, Maine	Vinalhaven, Maine
2-29-92	[Mary Dorothy]	F	Shields	William F.	Katie E. Duran	Shirley, Mass.	Portland, Maine
3-22-92	Arthur Eustus	M	Adams	William H.	Alfaretta Swaim	Davenport, England	Shelburne, N.S.
3-25-92		F	Donahue	John	Mary Fay	Ireland	Thomaston, Maine
4-1-92		M	Lotti	Rocco	Angelina Bottigi	Italy	Italy
8-23-92		F	Johnson	August	Christina Eleisson	Sweden	Sweden
10-31-92	Joseph	M	Miranda	Dominici	Josephine Lori	Italy	Italy
12-29-92	John O'Brien	M	Clancy	John O'Brien	Julia Rogers	Dublin, Ireland	Dublin, Ireland
1-11-93		M	Flemings	John McGrath	Ellen Jones	Watterford, Ireland	Bristol, Maine
2-28,93	Frances Kathleen	F	Hill	James A.	Bridget A. Rourke	Dublin, Ireland	Roscammon, Ireland
3-30-93		M	Morrison	Alexander	Maggie Roi	Banff, Scotland	Aberdeen, Scotland
5-7-93	Ezra	M	Cushing	Ezra J.	Julia Labour	St. Johnsbury, Vt.	Canada
8-8-93	Leonilda	F	Galasini	Giuseppe	Giacona Vanoni	Pelago, Italy	Pelago, Italy
11-4-93	Charles	M	Yokela	Mat	Lizzie Anderson	Finland	Finland
12-17-93		M	Miranda	Dominic	Josephine Lori	Italy	Italy
1-15-94	Joseph William	M	Shields	William	Catherine	Groton, Mass.	Portland, Maine
1-29-94	William Lorenzo	M	Bunker	Lorenzo P.	Sadie May King	Franklin, Maine	Topsham, Maine
2-25-94	Henry	M	Meldrum	William	Mary Gray	Aberdeen, Scotland	Aberdeen, Scotland
5-7-94	Julia	F	Clancy	John O'Brien	Julia Rogers	Dublin, Ireland	Dublin, Ireland
5-19-94		M	Landers	John T.	Mary A. Hobin	Rockland, Maine	Rockland, Maine
6-16,94	Dara	F	Cummings	Fred E.	Etta R. Haney	Augusta, Maine	Hancock, Maine
6-16-94		M	Hendricson	John	Edith Matson	Finland	Finland
7-15-94	Maggy S.	F	Milne	George	May Davis	Aberdeenshire	St. George, Maine
8-9-94		M	Markie	John	Mary Line-?	Finland	Finland
8-29-94	Angelina	F	DiBona	B.	Maria Tocci	Italy	Italy
9-10-94		F	Waterfield	Albert	Mary Gaitley	England	England
9-23-94		F	Leindblam	John	Wilda Fatmlof?	Sweden	Sweden
10-23-94		M	Patterson	Errastus P.	Margaret Duran	Rockland, Maine	Portland, Maine
11-12-94	Mary Jane	F	Ingraham	Richard	Jane Clark	Scotland	Scotland
2-23-95		M	Mattsan	R.	Ann Hendron?	Finland	Finland
3-15-95	none	F	Hill	James	Delia Rourke	Dublin, Ireland	Ireland
5-13-95	Alexander	M	Maitland	John	J. Southerland	Scotland	Scotland
7-3-95	Emma	F	Rehn	Andrew	C. Carlson	Sweden	Sweden
7-22-95	Agurthia	F	Landers	John T.	Mary A. Hobin	Rockland, Maine	Rockland, Maine
8-13-95	Charles	M	Espennett	Augustine	Angie Testa	Italy	Italy
9-2-95	Marian Frances	F	Nectora	Joseph A.	Jennie Patterson	Charleston, Mass.	Rockland
10-4-95	Robert G.	M	Meldrum	William	Mary Gray	Scotland	Scotland
11-19-95	Harry Harold	M	Lord	Joseph G.	Clara Wynn	St. George, N.B.	Ontario, Canada
11-29-95	[Beatrice Louise]	F	Shields	William	Kathrine Duran	Groton, Mass.	Portland, Maine
12-23-95	Roy	M	Rowling	Richard	Lucy F. Tighe	England	Rockland, Maine
12-30-95		M	Yokela	Matti	Kranwick	Finland	Finland
1-25-96		M	Gabrielson	William M.	Angie Benner	Norway	Round Pond, Maine
2-7-96	Mary Regis	F	Patterson	Erastus	Margaret Duran	Rockland, Maine	Portland, Maine
10-7-96	Alice	F	Clancy	John O'Brien	Julia Rogers	Dublin, Ireland	Dublin, Ireland
1-15-97		M	Johnson	Abraham	Lena Swanson	Sweden	Sweden
3-1-97	James Francis	M	Shields	William F.	Katherine Duran	Groton, Mass.	Portland, Maine
3-29-97	Flora	F	Kirkpatrick	John J.	Kate E. Mancy	Scotland	Monson, Mass.
4-10-97		F	Gabrielson	William Martin	Angie Benner	Norway, Europe	Bristol, Maine
4-10-97		F	Leedburg	Otto	Annie Johnson	Sweden	Sweden
5-1-97	(John Edward)	M	Nichols	Joseph A.	Jennie B. Patterson	Charlestown, Mass.	Rockland, Maine
5-15-97	Harold Edward	M	Rowling	William J.	Adeline Garrett	Rockland, Maine	Vinalhaven, Maine

*stillborn

Hurricane Island Record of Births 1892–1915

Date	Name	Sex	Last Name	Father	Mother's Maiden Name	Father's Birthplace	Mother's Birthplace
6-24-97	Edith Francis	F	Rehn	Andrew	Sophia Carlson	Sweden	Sweden
7-10-97		M	Minkginen	Otto	Amanta Kivesto	Finland	Finland
7-20-97		M	Landers	John T.	Mary A. Hobin	Rockland, Maine	Rockland, Maine
8-25-97	Alice Augusta	F	Carlson	Frank	Caroline Anderson	Sweden	Sweden
9-2-97		M	Yokela	Matt	Lizzie Anderson	Finland	Finland
10-2-97		M	Hill	James A.	Delia Rourke	Dublin, Ireland	Dublin, Ireland
10-2-97	Helen Elizabeth	F	Patterson	Erastus P.	Margaret M. Duran	Rockland, Maine	Portland, Maine
11-15-97		M	Swanson	John A.	Albine O. Holm	Sweden	Denmark
4-24-98	not named	F	Nelsen	Nels	Hana Nelsen	Sweden	Sweden
5-23-98	not named	F	Hendricksen	John	Edith Mattson	Finland	Finland
6-25-98	Margaret	F	Shields	William F.	Katherine Duran	Groton, Mass.	Portland, Maine
7-26-98		F	Murphy	Charles H.	Nellie F. Garrett	Andover, N.B.	Vinalhaven, Maine
8-10-98	Mary Adeline	F	Rowling	William J.	Addie M. Richards	Rockland, Maine	Vinalhaven, Maine
9-18-98		F	Gallisini	Giuseppi	Giacona Vanoni	Italy	Italy
10-4-98	John Martin	M	Rogers	John T.M.	Mary E. Rowling	Sharta, Ga.	Hurricane
10-4-98	Thomas Raymond	M	Landers	John T.	Mary A. Hobin	Rockland, Maine	Rockland, Maine
10-15-98		F	Meldrum	William	Mary Gray	Scotland	Scotland
10-24-98		M	Patterson	Erastus P.	Maggie M. Duran	Rockland, Maine	Portland, Maine
2-17-99		M	Swanson	John	Alberta Holm	Sweden	Denmark
4-7-99	Lyford William	M	Ross	James P.	Mary A. Duguid?	Scotland	Scotland
4-11-99	Marguerite Mary	F	Pratt	William	Maggie Williams	Scotland	Scotland
4-26-99	Amerigo Dewey	M	Gheccini?	Luigi	Richella Angella	Italy	Italy
4-29-99		M	Gabrielson	William Martin	Angie Benner	Scilisine, Norway	Round Pond, Maine
7-17-99	Grace	F	Shields	William F	Catharine Duran	Groton, Mass.	Portland, Maine
9-16-99	Thomas	M	McCormick	Archibald F.	Theresa F. Landers	New Brunswick	Hurricane Isle
11-3-99	Mary Theresa	F	Manning	William	Annie Donohue	Conway, Mass.	Ireland
11-21,99		M	Rogers	John M.	Mary E. Rowling	Sharta, Ga.	Hurricane
11-26-99	Myrtle Davis	F	Testa	Victoria	Lizzie Davis	Milan, Italy	St. George, Maine
11-29-99	Cecilia Antoinette	F	Bianchi	Angelo	Guiseppina Roiette	Italy	Italy
2-12-00	Gladys B	F	Poland	T.B.	Mildred Cusham?	Bristol, Maine	Friendship, Maine
2-16-00		M	Lawson	Eric A.	Sophia G. Carlson	Sweden	Sweden
2-19-00		M	Swanson	John	Albion Holm	Sweden	Denmark
6-5-00	Louise	F	Patterson	Erastus P.	Margaret M. Duran	Rockland, Maine	Portland, Maine
6-8-00	William	M	Glendenning	William H.	Mary A. Landers	Lachina, P.Q.	Rockland, Maine
7-1-00	Emg. Lovis	F	Nelson	Nels	Hanna Nelson	Sweden	Sweden
7-3-00		F	Smith	Alex E.	Isabelle Wilson	Scotland	Scotland
8-12-00	William L.	M	Vinal	Leonard W.	Mary J. Coyle	Vinalhaven, Maine	So. LaGrange, Maine
10-21-00		F	Hilding	Andrew	Lizzie Duncan	Sweden	Aberdeen, Scotland
1-4-01		F	Landers	John T.	Mary A. Hobin	Rockland, Maine	Rockland, Maine
2-19-01		M	Manning	William C.	Anna M. Donohue	Conway, Mass.	Ireland
3-9-01		F	Swanson	John	Albina Holm	Sweden	Denmark
5-10-01	Henry Rogers	M	Rogers	John T.M.	Mary E. Rowling	Sharta, Ga.	Hurricane
5-17-01	Victoria Felice	F	Simonelli	Alessandro	Cristino Foctu-?	Canara, Italy	Canara, Italy
5-25-01		F	Landers	Michael	Minnie A. Burns	Rockland, Maine	Vinalhaven, Maine
7-15-01	*	M	Johnson	August	Christina Elias	Sweden	Sweden
9-18-01	Dorothy	F	Patterson	Erastus P.	Maggie M. Duran	Rockland, Maine	Portland, Maine
12-5-01	Ralph A.	M	Glendenning	William H.	Mary A. Landers	Lachina, P.Q.	Rockland, Maine
12-23-01	Alma Munch	F	Munch	John	Sophia Mandolin	Finland	Finland
1-20-02		M	Testa	Vic	Josephine Canasi	Italy	Italy
2-8-02	Levanti	M	Coletti	Nunzio	Rosa DeBona	Italy	Italy
2-19-02		F	Ferrigno	Nicholas	Arnina? Esposito	Italy	Italy

*stillborn

Hurricane Island Record of Births 1892–1915

Date	Name	Sex	Last Name	Father	Mother's Maiden Name	Father's Birthplace	Mother's Birthplace
3-4-02		M	Manning	William C.	Anna Donohue	Conway, Mass.	Ireland
3-6-02		M	Ferrigno	Frank	Emily Falour	Italy	Italy
6-20-02	Antonio Donato	M	Fabrizio	Baetano	Rachela Ventre	Italy	Italy
7-9-02	Doris Isabelle	F	Nichols	Joseph	Jennie Patterson	Charlestown, Mass.	Rockland, Maine
11-5-02	Arthur	M	DiBona	Frank	Vingenza Panserall	Caserta, Italy	Caserta, Italy
12-3-02		F	Comolli	Stephenor	Mary Achli?	Italy	Italy
3-17-03		M	Baroffi	Louis	Pierina Massari	Italy	Italy
6-25-03	Florence Testa	F	Nichols	Joseph A.	Jennie Patterson	Charlestown, Mass.	Rockland, Maine
9-21-03	*	M	Landers	John T.	Mary Hobin	Rockland, Maine	Rockland, Maine
10-25-03		F	Ferrigno	Frank	Emelia Falour	Italy	Italy
12-10-03	William Louis	M	Ferrigno	Nicholas	Arnina? Esposito	Italy	Italy
12-16-03		M	Zoumoni	Ambrogia	Josephine Bittigi	Caserta, Italy	Caserta, Italy
1-14-04	Armido Pasqualin	M	Fabrizio	Gaetano	Rachela Ventre	Caserta, Italy	Caserta, Italy
2-25-04	Edith	F	Coletti	Nunzio	Rosa DiBona	Italy	Italy
6-17-04	Vival do Antonio	M	Berini	Luigi	Picol Geridetta	Shagnano Como, Italy	Shagnano Come, Italy
7-30-04	Luco DiBona	M	DiBona	Frank	Vingenza Calduci	San Donato, Italy	San Donato, Italy
7-26-04	Irene? Comolli	M	Comolli	Leonardo	Gensippina? Lotti	Italy	Italy
9-22-04		M	Bottinelli	Batasti	Minnie Caro	Italy	Italy
1-21-05	America Alpier	M	Molarini	James	Mary Cassini	Italy	Italy
3-3-05		M	Bariffo	Lourgi	Perina Masseri	Italy	Italy
5-6-05	Helen Isabell	F	Manning	William	Annie Donohue	Ireland	Ireland
7-19-05		M	Landers	John T.	Mary A. Hobin	Rockland, Maine	Rockland, Maine
7-26-05	Arthur Trogone	M	Trogone	Nicholas	Filomina Ferrigno	Italy	Italy
10-13-05		M	Berini	Louis	Picol Geridetta	Italy	Italy
11-11-05	Lino Gabrizo	F	Fabrizio	Gaetano	Rachela Ventre	Italy	Italy
9-8-05	Williamena	F	Douglas	Andrew H.	Maggie Morison	Scotland	Scotland
9-27-05		F	Garrett	Ralph	Adline Smith	Vinalhaven, Maine	Georgia
1-10-06	Ariniti	M	Quintilioma	Carmene	Loreta DiBona	Italy	Italy
2-1-06	T. McCormick	M	McCormick	A.F.	Teresa Landers	New Brunswick	Hurricane
3-12-06	Bella Rose	F	Coletti	Nunzio	Rosa DiBona	Italy	Italy
3-16-06	Dora C.	F	Landers	M.E.	M.A. Burns	Rockland, Maine	Vinalhaven, Maine
5-4-06		M	Mancius	Gracenti	Rita Gizza	Italy	Italy
4-30-06	Adelina DiBona	F	DiBona	Frank	Vingenca Colduci	Italy	Italy
1-4-07		M	Ferrigno	Frank	Emily Falour	Italy	Italy
3-5-07	Amelia	F	Fabrizio	Pasquale	Maritta Pagani	Italy	Italy
4-26-07	Filomena	F	Antonelli	Forunato	Castanza???	Italy	Italy
6-12-07	Libero	M	Coletti	Nunzio	Rosa DiBona	Italy	Italy
7-15-07	Johnnie	M	Abbatti	Antoni	Zoe Barsugli	Italy	Italy
7-21-07		M	Mancini	Libero	Giggi Mancini	Italy	Italy
7-23-07		F	Patterson	Edwin C.	Gertrude Landers	Rockland, Maine	Hurricane Isle
7-31-07	Aurora Grossi	F	Grossi	Siro	Formene Dinli??	Italy	Italy
9-20-07	Raymond Yule	M	Yule	William	Margaret Mennis	Scotland	Scotland
10-28-07	Nicola DeMartino	M	DeMartino	Giuseppi	Teresa Genchi	Italy	Italy
12-12-07	Helen Frances	F	Robinson	Eugene Palmer	Amie Eliza Rowlin	St. George, Maine	Hurricane
1-2-08		F	Allonson	Mathew	Herthie Bock-??	England	NewCastel, N.B.
2-5-08		M	Johnson	Charles	Julia Bergis	Sweden	Sweden
4-8-08		M	Busca?	Frank	Filomena Barru	Italy	Italy
5-10-08	Orelia Fabrizo	F	Fabrizo	Pasquale	M. Pagani	Italy	Italy
4-27-09	Anselmo Leone	M	Leone	Luccano	A. Centrona	Italy	Italy
7-13-09	Estircue Berini	F	Berini	Giuseppi	Marcia Trivebla	Italy	Italy
2-1-10	Elbert W.	M	Wentworth	A.G.	E.B. Rodd	Hanson, Maine	Boston, Mass.

*stillborn

Hurricane Island Record of Births 1892–1915

Date	Name	Sex	Last Name	Father	Mother's Maiden Name	Father's Birthplace	Mother's Birthplace
3-9-10		F	Grassi	Frank	Vedtina? Dallie?	Italy	Italy
3-13-10	Edmonda	F	Abiatti	Anthony	Zoie Barsugli	Italy	Italy
4-5-10	Junita	F	Larrabie	Georg	Gerogina Dickens	Union, Maine	W. Tremont, Maine
5-6-10	not given	M	Ferrigno	Frank	Emelia Flower	Italy	Italy
1-29-11	Charles Henry	M	Rowling	Chas. H.	Eugenia Pendleton	Hurricane Isle	Islesboro, Maine
3-31-11	*	M	Quintilini	N.	Asunta Coletti	Italy	Italy
3-21-11		M	Conway	Omer	Maud Haskell	Italy(?)	Italy(?)
4-23-11		M	Adinolfi	S.	Caterina? Alfini	Italy	Italy
6-4-11	Edith Baroffio	F	Baroffio	Luigi	Pierina Mossara	Italy	Italy
6-12-11	Archibald	M	Judkins	George	Myrtil Stanley	Stonington, Maine	Swans Island, Maine
7-31-11		M	Young	William P.	Alice M. Brown	Vinalhaven, Maine	Vinalhaven, Maine
8-14-11		F	Dalli	Frank	May Bell	Italy	Italy
8-24-11		F	Nilson	Gustave A.	Frances Patterson	Italy(?)	Italy(?)
4-25-12	Pearl	M	Philbrook	Ansel	Nellie Raymond	North Haven, Maine	Vinalhaven, Maine
4-1-13	Amos Dalli*	M	Dalli	Frank	May Lurebell	Italy	Italy
9-26-13		F	Abiatti	Antonio	Zoe Barsugli	Italy	Italy
9-3-14	Emilo	M	Tonetti	Henrico	Lacanio	Italy	Italy
3-23-15	Helen M. Ferrigno	F	Ferrigno	Frank	Emily Fiorella	Italy	Italy

*stillborn

Hurricane Island Record of Marriages 1896–1914

Date	Place	Names	Residence	Age	Occupation	Birthplace	No.	Father's Name	Mother's Name
9-23-96	Vinalhaven	Rowling, William J.	Hurricane	24	Granite Cutter	Rockland, Maine	2	Richard Rowling	Lucy F. Tighe
9-23-96	Vinalhaven	Richards, Addie M.	Hurricane	27		Vinalhaven	2	Truman F. Garrett	Emmeline Young
12-23-96	Vinalhaven	Rogers, J.T. Martin	Hurricane	23	Granite Cutter	Sparta, Ga.	1	James H. Rogers	Martha E. Martin
12-23-96	Vinalhaven	Rowling, Mary E.	Hurricane	18		Hurricane	1	Richard Rowling	Lucy F. Tighe
12-23-99	Hurricane	Hilding, Andrew	Hurricane	20	Granite Cutter	Sweden	1	John Hilding	Matilda Mannuson
1901	Hurricane	Testa, Vinchans	Hurricane	19	Granite Cutter	Italy	1	Jacob Testa	Grouilda Miluna?
1901	Hurricane	Rowling, Lilley	Hurricane	18		Hurricane	1	Richard Rowling	Lucy Tighe
1-29-03	Rockland	Rowling, R.O.	Hurricane	26	Granite Cutter	Hurricane	1	Richard Rowling	Lucy Tighe
1-29-03	Rockland	McInnis, Ellen	Vinalhaven	20	Domestic	Vinalhaven	1	John McInnis	Ellen Murry
4-13-03	Rockland	Trongone, Nicholas	Hurricane	20	Stonecutter	St. Michelle, Italy	1	Gaetano Trongone	Congetta DeVita
4-13-03	Rockland	Ferrigno, Rosa Filo	Hurricane	23	Dress Maker	Maiori, Italy	1	Raffaele Ferrigno	Maddalena Biango
6-23-04	Portland	Zorzi, Paolo	Hurricane	22	Granite Cutter	Italy	1	Telici Zorzi	Elizabeth Pelligrini
6-23-04	Portland	Zamoni, Margarita	Hurricane	22	Housekeeper	Italy	1	Ippi Zamoni	Maria Piatti
10-22-04	Vinalhaven	Dailey, Harry C.	Hurricane	23	Granite Cutter	Belfast, Maine	1	A.A. Dailey	Syphla Smith
10-22-04	Vinalhaven	Vinal, Bessie M.	Hurricane	20	Domestic	Vinalhaven, Maine	1	L. Vinal	Mary Coyle
3-10-05	Vinalhaven	Douglas, Andrew H.	Hurricane	22	Granite Cutter	Scotland	1	Andrew Douglas	Ann McKay
3-10-05	Vinalhaven	Morison, Maggie	Hurricane	16	Domestic	Scotland	1	Aleck Morison	Maggie Morison
6-21-05	S. Thomaston	Rowling, John	Hurricane	20	Granite Cutter	Hurricane Isle	1	Richard Rowling	Lucy Tighe
6-21-05	S. Thomaston	Clough, Edith	Hurricane	19	Domestic	Rockland	1	Hanson Clough	Florence Barker
8-19-05	Vinalhaven	Vinal, Fred C.	Hurricane	23	Tool Sharpener	Vinalhaven	1	Leonard W. Vinal	Mary S. Coyle
8-19-05	Vinalhaven	Wilson, Ethel M.	Hurricane	17	Domestic	Rockland, Maine	1	Chas. Wilson	Selma Rosland
1-17-06	Bucksport	Davis, David	Orland	21	Granite Cutter	South Dakota	1	John Davis	Marguerite Ried
1-17-06	Bucksport	McGrath, Mary E.	Hurricane	18	Domestic	Hurricane	1	John McGrath	Helen Jones
9-27-06	Thomaston	Robinson, E. Palmer	Hurricane	24	Granite Cutter	St. George, Maine	1	Solvenias Robinson	Lillias Robinson
9-27-06	Thomaston	Rowling, Annie E.	Hurricane	32	Domestic	Hurricane	1	Richard Rowling	Lucy Tighe
4-13-07	Rockland	Patterson, E.A.	Hurricane	27	Clerk	Rockland, Maine	1	John Patterson	Amanda Mitchell
4-13-07	Rockland	Landers, Gertrude	Hurricane	20	Domestic	Hurricane	1	J.F. Landers	Joana A. Sullivan
2-7-07	Rockland	Abbatti, Antoni	Hurricane	24	Granite Cutter	Italy	1	John Abbatti	Zanalli Rossi
2-7-07	Rockland	Barsugli, Zoe	Hurricane	22	Domestic	Italy	1	Antoni Barsugh	Casira Pinelli
5-22-07	Rockland	Neilson, Gustav A.	Hurricane	39	Granite Cutter	Sweden	1	John Neilson	Nellie Hanson
5-22-07	Rockland	Patterson, Frances	Hurricane	33	Domestic	Rockland, Maine	1	John Patterson	Amanda Mitchell
7-10-07	Rockland	Brusa, Frank	Hurricane	25	Granite Cutter	Italy	1	Luigi Brusa	Gorimana Calduor
7-10-07	Rockland	Barsugli, Filemino	Hurricane	20	Domestic	Italy	1	Anthony Barsugli	Cesira Pinelli
8-28-07	Vinalhaven	Searles, William A.	Hurricane	43	Painter	Rockland, Maine	2	William F. Searles	Elona Miller
8-28-07	Vinalhaven	Conway, Blanche	Hurricane	22	Domestic	Hurricane	1	R.Y. Conway	Emma J. Haskell
10-10-07	Vinalhaven	Conway, Ernest O.	Hurricane	27	Engineer	Vinalhaven	1	Rufus Y. Conway	Annie B. Young
10-10-07	Vinalhaven	Haskell, Maud	Hurricane	16	Domestic	Vinalhaven	1	Daniel F. Haskell	Catherine Eaton
10-30-07	Rockland	Burpee, Charles W.	Rockland	22	Machinist	Rockland	1	Charles E. Burpee	Isebel F. Birch
10-30-07	Rockland	Bonn?, Evelyn M.	Hurricane	23	Nurse	Rockland	1	John Bonn	Ann Keenan
12-31-08	Rockland	Quintiani, Nicola	Hurricane	23	Granite Cutter	Italy	1	Clementini Quintian	Costanza Musselli
12-31-08	Rockland	Coletti, Assunta	Hurricane	19	Domestic	Italy	1	Nunzio Coletti	Rosa DiBona
3-24-10	Rockland	Smith, Alexander	Hurricane	51	Blacksmith	Scotland	2	George Smith	Catherine Cheper?
3-24-10	Rockland	Morison, Marguerite	Hurricane	49	Laundress	Scotland	2	James Pate	Marguerite Allen
5-1-10	Vinalhaven	Waldron, Maynard	Hurricane	23	Granite Cutter	Frankfort, Maine	1	Charles Waldron	Della C. Jones
5-1-10	Vinalhaven	Larrabee, Emily N.	Waldoboro	19	At Home	Waldoboro, Maine	1	Alonzo Larrabee	Harriet A. Wyman
9-3-10	Rockland	Dalli, Frank	Hurricane	30	Quarryman	Italy	1	Anesto Dalli	Matildi Tini
9-3-10	Rockland	Lucibello, Mary	Hurricane	22	Housekeeper	Italy	1	Luigi Lucibello	L. Benativoglio
9-9-14	Rockland	Kegan, Edward J.	Thompson, Ct.	39	Supt., Woolen Mill	Chepachet, R.I.	1	Lawrence Keegan	Elizabeth Fagan
9-9-14	Rockland	Shields, Mary D.	Hurricane	22	Teacher	Hurricane Isle	1	William F. Shields	Catherine C. Duran

Hurricane Island Record of Deaths 1892–1914

Date	Cause of Death	Name of Deceased	Age	Place of Birth	Sex	Married?	Occupation
5-3-92	Suicide – razor wound	Landers, Robert Jr.	35		M	Widowed	Stone Polisher
1-7-94	Pneumonia	Hawley, Michael	84	Ireland	M		Laborer
7-28-94	Appendicitis	Cummings, Sara E.	7	Hancock, Maine	F		
8-27-94	Congestion bands	Jacobson, Eliza Mary	1 mo.	Hurricane	F		
8-29-94	Colera infantue	Bunker, Willie L.	6 mo.	Hurricane	M		
12-1-94	Drowned	Waterfield, Albert	34	England	M	Married	Paving Cutter
7-19-95	Aneurism of Aorta	Jospehson, Charles	24	Finland	M	Single	Paving Cutter
9-16-95	Bright's Disease	Lane, Maria	29	Tsakyes	F	Married	
1-1-96	Spinal Meningitis	Murphy, Jerrold T.	2 mo.	Vinalhaven	M		
2-6-96	Old Age	Galicini, Mrs.		Italy	F	Widowed	Domestic
6-12-96	Consumption	Shields, Moses F.	60	New York City	M	Married	Stone Cutter
7-22-97	Pentonitis	Minkginen, Amanda	19	Finland	F	Married	
9-1-97	Cholera Infantum	Rowling, Harold E.	3 mo.	Hurricane	M		
1-22-98	Bronchial Pneumonia	Shields, James F.	10 mo.	Hurricane	M		
1-22-98	Convulsions	Rehn, Andrew	45	Sweden	M		
9-7-98	Phthisis	Garrett, Irneman F.	61	Vinalhaven	M	Married	Stone Cutter
2-25-99	Phthisis	Rolfe, Elbridge	66	Vinalhaven	M	Married	Stone Cutter
3-21-99	Strangulation	Swanson, Charlie	5 days	Hurricane	M	Single	
4-14-00	Manition	Mitchell, David M.	83	Paris, Maine	M	Widowed	Carpenter
11-5-00		Hilding, no name	15 days	Hurricane	F	Single	
11-30-00	evidently Heart Disease	Butler, Jennie S.	44	Vinalhaven	F	Married	Housewife
11-26-00	Accidental Fall out of window	Daley, John	34	Lanesville, Mass.	M	Single	Granite Cutter
5-10-01	Premature birth	Rogers, Henry	6 hours	Hurricane	M	Single	
10-6-01	Broncho Pneumonia	Lawson, Erik A.**	1	Hurricane	M	Single	
11-26-01	Fhethias	Smith, Isabella	39	Scotland	F	Married	Housewife
1-3-02	Quanition	Patterson, Dorothy	3 mo.	Hurricane	F	Single	
4-16-02	General disability	Vincent, Stephen	69	Cornwall, England	M	Widowed	Stone Cutter
6-13-02	Senility	Young, Jeremiah P.	87	Islesborough	M	Widowed	Common Laborer
1-4-02	Spinal Meningitis	Smith, Mary Olive	2	Hurricane	F	Single	
10-12-02	Pneumonia	Webster, William**	52	Aberdeen, Scotland	M	Married	Paving Cutter
3-27-03	Appcndicitis	Landers, Dorio Isabella	13	Hurricane	F	Single	
9-22-03	Instrument birth	Landers, no name		Hurricane Isle		Single	
9-19-04	Old Age	Kirkpatrick, Hollis	81	Rockland, Maine	M	Widowed	Stone Mason
12-11-05	Cerebral Hemorrage	Conway, Annie J.	53	Vinalhaven	F	Widowed	Housewife
12-11-05	Telampia Pertustio	Fabrigo, no name	1 mo.	Hurricane	F	Single	
6-7-06	Pulmonary Faberedines	Smith, Adline**	19	Lithonia, Ga.	F	Single	Housekeeper
7-16-06	Heart Failure	Copeland	57	Scotland	M	Single	Granite Cutter
1-14-07	Acute Nepleretes	Hindkerson, Ida	18 days	Vinalhaven	F	Single	
3-10-07	Acute Rheumatism	Mitchell, Fannie H.	58	Rockland, Maine	F	Single	Servant
4-30-07	Tuberculosis Meningitis	Smith, Isabella	1	Hurricane	F	Single	
5-5-07	Rheumatism of Heart	Ferrigno, Romeo	12	Boston, Mass.	M	Single	Student
7-15-07	Premature birth	Abbatti, Johnnie	1 day	Hurricane	M	Single	
9-14-07	Pulmonary Tuberculosis	Rowling, Richard	62	Hurricane??	M	Married	Foreman
12-30-07	Malformation of heart	Allison, Matchew	12 hours	Hurricane	M	Single	
2-5-08	Malformation	Johnson, no name		Hurricane	M		
3-4-08	Psthisis	Keay, George S.	22	Aberdeen, Scotland	M	Single	Blacksmith
3-24-08	Pulmonary Tuberculosis	Smith, James R.	19	Aberdeen, Scotland	M	Single	Laborer
9-30-08	Accidental drowning	Smith, George G.	57	North Haven	M	Single	Fisherman
8-8-09	Intestinal obstruction	Larrabee, George W.	6 mo.		M	Single	
1-21-10	Phthisis	Hilding, Mathilda	56	Sweden	M?	Married	Housewife
3-10-10	Chronic Bright's Disease	Waldron, Charles L.	52	Frankfort, Maine	M	Married	Granite Cutter
12-?-11	Senile gangrene	Sullivan, Bridget Wall	83	Ireland	F	Widowed	Housekeeper
4-2-13	Stillborn	Dalli, Amos	0	Hurricane	M		

DEPARTMENT OF THE ARMY
UNITED STATES MILITARY ACADEMY
WEST POINT. NEW YORK 10996

July 20, 1988

REPLY TO
ATTENTION OF

USMA Archives

Ms. Eleanor M. Richardson
34 Fletcher Street
Kennebunk, Maine 04043

Dear Ms. Richardson:

I am in receipt of your letter of July 6, 1988.

Having now had a bit more time to research the case of Cadet Davis Tillson, I can provide you with additional information on his tenure as a U.S. Military Academy Cadet.

I am enclosing a typescript of the letter from the Superintendent to the Chief Engineer outlining Tillson's case. In the letter, the Superintendent recommends that Tillson be allowed to remain at the Academy to continue his studies. He also states that Tillson expects to be ready to take his final exams in August.

The scenario presented by the Superintendent in his letter was played out. Tillson was allowed to remain at the Academy. He was examined by the Academic Board on August 30, 1850, and was found to be proficient. He was placed twenty-third in his class of seventy-four members in Mathematics, thirty-fourth in English, and forty-eighth in French.

Tillson went on to complete his third class (sophmore) year at the Academy. He was ranked tenth in a class of sixty-three members after the June examinations in 1851. Tillson resigned from the Academy on September 25, 1851.

I hope this information will be helpful. If we can be of any further assistance, please do not hesitate to contact us.

Sincerely,

Suzanne Christoff
Assistant Archivist, USMA

Enclosure

U.S. Military Academy
West Point, New York
May 30, 1850

Brig. General Joseph G. Totten
Chief Engineer
Washington, D.C.

Sir:

I have the honor to transmit, herewith, the report of Dr. S.M. Cuyler, Surgeon of the post, in the case of Cadet Tillson of the 4th Class.

Cadet Tillson was taken on the sick report for pain in the foot on the 14th of December last, although he has since stated his foot gave him some trouble whilst he was in camp. On the 18th of December he returned to duty, but was again taken on the sick report on the 24th of the same month for sprain, and was finally admitted into the hospital on the 2nd of January following, where he remained under treatment until the 21st of March last, when he was removed by the Surgeon to the city of New York, and from thence to the U.S. Hospital at Governors island. On the 23rd of March the diseased portion of the limb was removed as stated by the Surgeon. Cadet Tillson remained at the hospital on Governors island attended by the Surgeon of that post, and visited by the Medical Officers of this as often as their duties here would permit, until the 28th of April, when he was sufficiently restored to be brought back to the Academy, and is now in the hospital so far convalescent as to be enabled to walk with the aid of crutches. I now present the case of Cadet Tillson to the department and the authorities at Washington, in reference to his being permitted to remain at the Academy for the purpose of pursuing his studies, which he is very solicitous of doing. He passed his probationary examination last January in a very creditable manner, his standing being 13 in Mathematics, 11 in English studies, and 10 in General Merit. The conduct of Cadet Tillson has been very good since his connection with the institution. Having only 10 demerits recorded against him at this time for the academic year. He has borne his long confinement and sickness with great patience and fortitude and has commended himself by his general good behavior and manly deportment to the good opinion of the authorities of the Academy. I beg leave therefore respectfully to recommend his case to the favorable consideration of the department and the honorable Secretary of the War.

As Cadet Tillson has been unable to study but little since the month of December, he could not pass his examination next month, even if his health at this time permitted his attendance at it, but he thinks he could prepare himself sufficiently during the summer to be examined at the close of August, so as to pursue his studies with his class the next term.

Signed,

/s/

Henry Brewerton
Capt.: Corps of Engrs.
Supt., Military Academy

Bibliography

"Acts and resolves of the 57th Legislature of the State of Maine," Augusta, Sprague, Owen & Nash, printers to the State, 1878, p. 27.

"Acts and Resolves of the 100th Legislature of the State of Maine," Augusta, 1921, Chapter 89, p. 413.

"Acts and Resolves of the 116th Legislature of the State of Maine," 1937, Chapter 36, p. 400.

Annual Reports of the State Superintendent of Common Schools, State of Maine, Augusta, State Printers, 1878–1914.

Art Work of Knox County, Maine, published in nine parts, by W.H. Parish Publishing Co., 1895. Parts 5 and 7.

Bangor Daily News, July 27, 1971, article by Dennis Mills, "It's a School of Hard Knocks on Island Off Penobscot Bay."

Beacom, Seward E., *Silent Fingers of Faith,* A History of the Churches of North Haven, Maine, 1784 – 1981. Published by the North Haven (Maine) Historical Society, 1981, p. 83.

Blanchard, Fessenden S., *Ghost Towns of New England,* N.Y., Dodd, Mead & Co., 1960, pp. 142–145.

Boston Sunday Post, Boston, Mass.
October 29, 1916, p. 48, Article by John Coggswell, "New England's Lost Town Discovered."
July 30, 1922, p. 49, Article by J.C. Wade, "Once Populous, Now Deserted Village."

Bureau of Industrial and Labor Statistics for the State of Maine, Augusta, 1887.

Caldwell, Bill, *Islands of Maine, Where America really began,* Portland, Maine, Guy Gannett Publishing Co., 1981.

Colorado Outward Bound School, *Colorado Outward Bound School,* brochure, 1963.

Commissioner of Industrial and Labor Statistics, 1887, and 1907, pp. 7 and 469–470.

Conkling, Philip W., *Islands In Time – A Natural and Human History of the Islands of Maine,* Camden, Maine, Down East Books, 1981.

Cyclopaedia of American Biography, New York, D. Appleton & Co., 1889, p. 119.

Dale, T. Nelson, *The Commercial Granites of New England,* Washington, D.C., Government Printing Office, 1923, pp. 5, 6, 148–50.

Down East Magazine, March 1988, article by James P. Brown "Outward Bound with Bob Rheault," pp. 36–40.

Duncan, Roger; Blanchard, F.; Ware, John, *A Cruising Guide to the New England Coast,* N.Y., Dodd, Mead, & Co., 1961, p. 342.

Elkins, L. Whitney, *Coastal Maine,* Bangor, Me., The Hillsborough Co., 1924, p. 279.

Fuller, Nathan, ed., *The Down East Reader,* N.Y. and Philadelphia, J.B. Lippincot Co., 1962, pp. 40–43: "Life and Death of an Island," by M. Shea.

Gaston, Thomas, "Hurricane Island," term paper written at Harvard University, May 1, 1961, in collections of the Maine Historical Society.

Godfrey, Robert, *Outward Bound: Schools of the Possible,* Garden City, N.Y., Anchor Press/Doubleday, 1980.

Grindle, Roger, *Tombstones and Paving Blocks, The History of the Maine Granite Industry,* Rockland, Maine, a Courier of Maine Book, 1977.

Hurricane Island Birth, Marriage and Death records, 1892–1914 (see appendix), in town clerk's office, Vinalhaven, Maine.

Hurricane Island Outward Bound School, Catalog of Courses, 1988, Rockland, Maine.

Knox Lands, Vol. 26, p. 412; Vol. 27, pp. 10–11 and p. 96; Vol. 39, p. 163; Vol. 33, p. 203; Vol. 31, p. 16; Vol. 40, p. 168; Vol. 48, p. 643; Vol. 148, p. 373; Vol. 150, p. 302; Vol. 188, p. 101; and Vol. 249, p. 448 in Knox County Court House, Rockland, Maine.

Maine Granite Quarries and Prospects, Maine Geological Survey, John R. Rand, State Geologist, published by the Dept. of Economic Development in Augusta on May 1, 1958.

Maine Register, State Year-Book and Legislative Manuals, 1878–1925, published annually, prepared pursuant to orders of the Legislature. Compiled and published by Grenville M. Donham, Portland (1900 ed.).

Maine Town and Census Records, on file in Maine State Archives, Augusta. U.S. Census, 1880, 1890, 1900 and 1910.

McLane, Charles B., *Islands of the Mid-Maine Coast: Penobscot and Blue Hill Bays,* Kennebec Press, Woolwich, Maine, pp. 103–109.

Munson, Gorham, *Penobscot,* Down East Paradise, J.B. Lippincot Co., N.Y. and Philadelphia, 1959, pp. 183–184.

New York Times, May 1, 1895, p. 5 col. 5, obituary for Gen. Davis Tillson.

Reports of the State Board of Health of the State of Maine, Augusta, 1885–1905.

Rich, Louise Dickinson, *State O'Maine,* A Regions of America book, New York, Harper and Row, 1964.

The Rockland Courier-Gazette, Feb. 19, 1889; April 23, 1889; obituary for Davis Tillson, May 7, 1895; Aug. 18, 1896; Tuesday, Nov. 10, 1914; obituary for John T. Landers, November 24, 1914. Series of three articles by Dick Dooley, Aug. 19, Aug. 28, and Sept. 4, 1975, Rockland Gazette, Feb. 12, 1880, p. 1.

Rockland Opinion, Nov. 3, 1876; Nov. 10, 1876; Nov. 14, 1876, p. 2; Dec. 1, 1876, pp. 1–2; Dec. 8, 1876, pp. 2–3; Dec. 22, 1876, p. 2; Dec. 29, 1876, p. 2; Jan. 12, 1877; Jan. 26, 1877, p. 4; Feb. 16, 1877, p. 2; Feb. 23, 1877; June 15, 1877, p. 2; June 22, 1877, p. 2; June 29, 1877, p. 2; July 6, 1877, p. 2; Obituary for Davis Tillson, May 3, 1895, p. 2.

Rutherford, Phillip R., *The Dictionary of Maine Place Names,* the Bond Wheelright Co., Freeport, ME 1970.

Shore Village Story, An Informal History of Rockland, Maine published by the Rockland Bicentennial Committee, 1976, printed the Courier-Gazette.

Simpson, Dorothy, *The Maine Islands in Story and Legend,* J.B. Lippincot Co., N.Y., 1960.

The Tillson Genealogy, from Edmon Tilson at Plymouth, New England, 1638 to 1911, with brief sketches of the family in England back to 1606, Baltimore, Gateway Press, 1982.

Vinal, Harold, *Hurricane, A Maine Coast Chronicle,* Brattleboro, Stephen Daye Press, 1936.

Vinalhaven Centennial Committee, *A Brief History of Vinalhaven,* 1889.

Vinalhaven Echo, Nov. 10, 1887–Jan. 24, 1889.

Vinalhaven Town Records, Vol. 3, March 2, 1874; Feb. 20, 1875; Feb. 27, 1875; March 6, 1876; Nov. 7, 1876, in Maine State Archives, Augusta.

Vinalhaven Town Reports, 1877–1889, in Vinalhaven Library.

Winslow, Sidney, "Intimate View of Vinalhaven," a series of articles in the Rockland Courier Gazette, Rockland, Maine, 1944–45.

Winslow, Sidney L., *Fish Scales and Stone Chips,* Machigonne Press, Portland, ME, 1952, pp. 73–74.

Young, Hazel, *Islands of New England,* Boston, Little, Brown & Co., 1954, pp. 82–83.

INTERVIEWS

Mrs. Minnie Vinal Chilles, Vinalhaven, Maine
Childhood on Hurricane Island, 1900–1905
Interviewed at Mrs. Chilles' home, October 19, 1963, 7:00 p.m.

Mr. and Mrs. Leslie Dyer, Vinalhaven, Maine
Hurricane Island
Interviewed at their home, Saturday, Oct. 19, 1963, 4:00 p.m.

Capt. Charles Philbrook, interviewed at the Ferry Landing, Vinalhaven, Me.
    Childhood on Hurricane Island, ca. 1925.
    Interviewed at Vinalhaven Ferry Landing, Oct. 20, 1963, 12:15 p.m.

Mr. Peter Willauer, Groton, Mass.
    A new Outward Bound School on Hurricane Island
    Interviewed at Groton School, Oct. 26, 1963.

Mrs. Margaret Philbrook Smith, Eliot, Maine
    Childhood on Hurricane Island, 1917–1922
    Interviewed at her home, March 26, 1988

Mrs. Mary Olson, Vinalhaven, Maine
    Her mother's childhood on Hurricane Island
    Interviewed at her home, March 24, 1988.

Mr. Buz Tripp, Tenants' Harbor, Maine
    Archeological finds and photos of Hurricane's early days
    Interviewed March 25, 1988 and Aug. 15, 1988 at Hurricane Island
    Outward Bound School, Rockland, Penobscot Bay, and Hurricane Island

Index

Facing page:
Tillson realized early that there was more profit to be made in finishing the stone than from quarrying it. Stone was sent from many other quarries to be finished by Italian stonecutters at these cutting sheds. Photo courtesy of HIOBS.

About the Author

Eleanor Motley Richardson, a fourth generation summer resident of North Haven, Maine, has written three local histories – *Hurricane Island, North Haven Summers,* and *Andover, A Century of Change 1896-1996.* The author began researching the history of Hurricane Island in 1963 as a junior at the Winsor School in Boston and 25 years later painstakingly assembled this priceless visual and narrative history of Hurricane's granite community. She is now an organ builder for the Andover Organ Company in Lawrence, Massachusetts, and music director at the Unitarian Universalist Congregation in Andover, where her husband, Peter, is the minister.